Bill Taylor
makes
Desserts

THE CROSSING PRESS
FREEDOM, CALIFORNIA

For information on bulk purchases or group discounts for this and other Crossing Press titles, please contact our Special Sales Manager at 800/777-1048.
Visit our Web site: **www.crossingpress.com**

Library of Congress Cataloging-in-Publication Data

Taylor, Bill (Robert William)
    Bill Taylor makes desserts / by Bill Taylor.
        p. cm.
    Includes index.
    ISBN 1-58091-069-6 (pbk.)
    1. Dessetts. I. Title.

    TX773.T385   2000
    641.8'6--dc21   99-089633

Contents

Chapter 1

Cookies, Brownies, & Bars   5

Chapter 2

Pies & Cobblers   45

Chapter 3

Cakes, Frostings, & Fillings   81

Chapter 4

Coffee Cakes & Dessert Breads   115

Chapter 5

Desserts You Eat with a Spoon   127

Cookies, Brownies, & Bars

As everyone knows, cookies can be enjoyed at any time, in the lunch bag, after school or work, as a mid-afternoon snack, or the finishing touch to dinner. They are easy to make, and with the right equipment, they take hardly any time at all. Most cookie dough freezes satisfactorily so large batches can be made up ahead of time.

I make a lot of cookies at Crossing Press for lunch, or just to have around for late afternoon snacks. Whenever we have a party or some kind of event that calls for food, I make sure there are heaping trays of cookies. Here are some tips I've been able to pick up along the way.

- Read the recipe thoroughly before you begin and have the equipment and ingredients ready to go.
- Most cookie recipes call for cookie sheets. Use nice shiny ones or cover your old pans with aluminum foil. They reflect heat better and the cookie will bake more evenly. Sheets that have darkened with time will absorb heat faster and burn the cookies too quickly on the bottom and around the edges.
- Grease a cookie sheet only if the recipe calls for it. Too much fat infused into the cookie dough makes it spread out too much.
- If you use an insulated sheet (air between two sheets of aluminum), you may find that the baking time increases slightly.
- When I specify brown sugar, I mean dark brown sugar. Brown sugar, either the light or dark variety, is always measured packed down into the measuring cup.
- I've learned to use a timer because I usually have more than one thing going on at once. Cookies can overbake if cooked

for just a minute too long. But whether you use a timer or not, always check the cookies near the end of the baking time to see if they need to come out early.

- Check your oven regularly with an oven thermometer. If the oven temperature is off, have it adjusted or adjust the cooking time to compensate. Too hot an oven can ruin a batch of cookies. Know the idiosyncrasies of your oven. Some have hot spots, or won't heat up to the temperature they are set for.
- Don't put cookie dough on a hot sheet. If the dough is set on a warm sheet, it can start to spread or bake before it goes in the oven.
- I usually work with several sheets at a time and rotate them.
- Always use the middle racks in the oven and, most important, always preheat the oven before baking.
- I always taste the dough before I bake it to make sure the spicing is right.
- Always sit down and sample a cookie or two straight out of the oven, with a cup of coffee or a large glass of milk.

Bars

This is the best way to produce uniform bars.
- Use a pan with a 2-inch rim or higher. Most bar cookies are baked in standard square or rectangular pans. The most common sizes are the 8-inch square, 9-inch square, and the 9- x 13-inch rectangle. Remember, the bigger the pan, the dryer the bar will be. The smaller the pan, the moister it will be.
- When bars come out of the oven, cool them right in the pan. Set the pan on a wire rack so there is good air circulation under and around the pan.
- Bars are best stored in the pan, wrapped with plastic for the short term. For long-term storage, wrap each bar individually. They are then ready for storing, freezing, or sending off in a lunch box.
- Have everything ready to go before starting a recipe and preheat the oven before baking.

Brownies

I tried for years to come up with the perfect brownie recipe. One day it occurred to me that I had half a dozen great recipes and therefore ought to quit searching and just enjoy what I had. In this section of the book, I've included the best of those recipes. Here are a couple of tips to improve any brownie recipe:

• If you can, resist cutting into the brownies until they've had a chance to cool down to room temperature. You'll find cutting them will be much easier, and the taste and texture will improve.

• If you find a recipe you really like, always follow that recipe to the letter.

Easy & Fast Buttery Cookies

I like these with bowls of fresh red raspberries and cream.

*Makes
3 dozen
sugar cookies
or
1 1/2 dozen
sandwiches*

1/2 cup butter-flavored vegetable shortening

3/4 cup sugar

1 1/2 tablespoons milk

1 egg

1/2 teaspoon vanilla

1 cup plus 3 tablespoons all-purpose flour

1/4 teaspoon salt

1/4 teaspoon baking powder

1/4 cup butter, melted

1 Preheat the oven to 375° F.

2 Cream the shortening, sugar, and milk until light and fluffy.

3 Beat the egg with the vanilla.

4 Combine the flour, salt, and baking powder. Mix into the creamed mixture and beat until smooth.

5 Drop the dough by the tablespoonful onto a nonstick cookie sheet about 2 inches apart.

6 Bake the cookies for 9 minutes, or until they are golden at the edges.

7 Remove from the oven and brush the cookies with melted butter. Remove them to a flat surface to cool.

On the next page you will find three ways to gild the lily. You can frost them, glaze them, or fill them. Or you can put together a sandwich with frosting, filling, and glaze.

Variations

Vanilla Frosting

1/2 cup butter

4 cups powdered sugar

1/3 cup milk

1 teaspoon vanilla

Combine all the ingredients in a small bowl and beat at low speed until mixed, then high speed until smooth and creamy. This frosting works well in a pastry bag.

Chocolate Glaze

1 1/2 cups semisweet chocolate chips

2 teaspoons butter

Chopped nuts or sprinkles

Combine the chips and the butter and melt at a very low heat in a double boiler, stir well. Cool slightly, then dip one end of the cookie halfway up in the chocolate. Before the chocolate hardens, you can sprinkle it with finely chopped nuts or sprinkles. Place the cookies on waxed paper until the chocolate is firm.

Chocolate Filling

1/3 cup butter

3/4 cup cocoa

1/4 teaspoon salt

1/2 cup milk

2 teaspoons vanilla

4 cups powdered sugar

Melt the butter over low heat. Remove from the stove and add the cocoa and salt. Mix well. Mix in the milk and vanilla. Blend in the sugar one cup at a time. Mix until smooth and creamy. Add more sugar to thicken or more milk to thin. Spread the filling on the bottom of half of the cookies. Top with the remaining cookies. Gently press together.

Fast Wheat Germ Cookies

This recipe is really tasty. I use pecans here, but any nut will do the job as well. This recipe can be doubled and the cookies stored in an airtight container for several days.

Makes 3 dozen **1 package yellow cake mix**

1 egg

3 tablespoons brown sugar

1/4 cup oil

2 tablespoons butter, melted

3/4 cup wheat germ

2 tablespoons water

3/4 cup chopped pecans

1 Preheat the oven to 375° F.

2 Combine the cake mix, egg, brown sugar, oil, butter, wheat germ, and water in a bowl. Blend well and stir in the nuts.

3 Drop the dough by the tablespoonful on a nonstick cookie sheet.

4 Bake the cookies for 10 minutes if you like them soft, or 12 minutes for crispy cookies.

5 Cool for a minute or so on the cookie sheet and then remove to a flat surface to cool completely.

Poppy Seed Cookies

I love poppy seeds in breads, cakes, and cookies. These cookies are light and fluffy and taste of almonds. Cook them until they are just golden.

Makes 3 dozen

3/4 cup sugar

1/3 cup vegetable shortening

2 tablespoons light corn syrup

1 1/4 teaspoons almond extract

1 egg

2 1/4 cups all-purpose flour

2 tablespoons poppy seeds

1 teaspoon baking soda

1 Preheat the oven to 350° F.

2 Cream the sugar with the shortening until light and fluffy.

3 Add the corn syrup, almond extract, and egg. Mix well.

4 Combine the flour, poppy seeds, and baking soda. Add to the sugar mixture and blend until smooth.

5 Drop the dough by the tablespoonful on a nonstick cookie sheet and bake for about 10 minutes. The cookies should be light gold in color, not brown.

6 Cool the cookies for a couple of minutes and then remove them to a flat surface.

Southern Brown Sugar Cookies

This cookie is from an old recipe my great-grandmother handed down to her daughter, my grandma, who gave it to me when she found out I was interested in baking.

Makes 3 dozen

1 cup brown sugar

1/4 cup water

1/4 cup honey

1 egg

2 1/3 cups all-purpose flour

1 cup coarsely ground pecans

1 tablespoon baking soda

2 teaspoons ground cinnamon

1/2 teaspoon ground allspice

1/4 teaspoon salt

1 Preheat the oven to 350° F.

2 Combine the sugar, water, honey, and egg. Beat at high speed until mixed well. Set aside.

3 Combine the flour, pecans, baking soda, cinnamon, allspice, and salt. Then combine both mixtures.

4 Drop the batter on a nonstick cookie sheet by the teaspoonful about 1 1/2 inches apart.

5 Bake the cookies for 10 to 12 minutes, or until they are lightly browned on the edges.

6 Give the spices the time to mellow, optionally a half hour if you can wait that long.

New England Maple Cookies

I love these with hot cocoa or a cup of espresso.

Makes 3 dozen   **1 cup brown sugar**

1/2 cup vegetable shortening

1 1/2 teaspoons maple extract

1 teaspoon vanilla extract

2 eggs

2 cups all-purpose flour

1 teaspoon baking soda

1/2 teaspoon ground cinnamon

1/4 teaspoon ground allspice

1/8 teaspoon ground cloves

1/8 teaspoon ground cardamom

1   Preheat the oven to 325° F.

2   Cream the sugar and the shortening until light and fluffy.

3   Add both the maple and vanilla extracts and eggs. Beat until smooth and creamy.

4   Combine the flour, baking soda, cinnamon, allspice, cloves, and cardamom. Mix well.

5   Drop the dough by the tablespoonful onto a nonstick cookie sheet.

6   Bake the cookies for 10 minutes.

7   Cool the cookies on the baking sheet for a couple of minutes, then move them to a flat surface to cool completely.

Peanut Butter Cookies

This recipe makes exceptional cookies. I'd advise doubling the recipe.

Makes 2 dozen
1/2 cup vegetable shortening

1 cup peanut butter

1 cup sugar

1/4 cup brown sugar

1 teaspoon vanilla

1 egg

1 1/4 cups all-purpose flour

1 teaspoon baking soda

1/2 teaspoon baking powder

1/4 teaspoon salt

1 Preheat the oven to 375° F.

2 Cream the shortening, peanut butter, both sugars, and vanilla until well blended.

3 Beat in the egg.

4 Combine the flour, baking soda, baking powder, and salt.

5 Combine both mixtures.

6 Drop the batter by the tablespoonful onto a nonstick cookie sheet. Dip a fork in flour and flatten the cookies in a crisscross pattern.

7 Bake for 8 to 10 minutes.

8 Cool the cookies in the pan for several minutes. Remove to a flat surface to finish cooling.

Peanutty Chocolate Cookies

If you like peanut butter and chocolate, this is a perfect recipe for you to try. The peanuts can be Spanish or Virginia, with skins on or off, dry roasted or fried in oil. It doesn't matter. Use whatever you like to eat.

Makes 3 dozen

1/2 cup all-purpose flour

1/2 cup cocoa

1/2 teaspoon baking soda

1/2 teaspoon salt

1/2 cup peanut butter, at room temperature

1/2 cup butter

3/4 cup sugar

1/2 cup brown sugar

1 egg

1/4 cup milk

1 cup chopped, roasted peanuts

1 Preheat the oven to 375° F.

2 Sift together the flour, cocoa, baking soda, and salt.

3 Cream the peanut butter and butter. Add both the sugars and mix well.

4 Beat in the egg.

5 Add the dry ingredients to the sugars alternating with the milk. Stir in the peanuts.

6 Drop the dough by the tablespoonful onto a nonstick cookie sheet. Bake for 12 to 14 minutes. Cool on a flat surface.

Chocolate Chip Cookies

I've tried a lot of chocolate chip cookie recipes, but this one seems to be everybody's favorite. You can substitute butter or margarine for the vegetable shortening, but I've found shortening makes a flakier cookie. This recipe can be doubled, and the cookies stored in an airtight container for several days.

Makes 3 dozen   **1/2 cup vegetable shortening**

3/4 cup brown sugar

1 egg

2 tablespoons vanilla extract

1/2 cup chopped dates

1 cup all-purpose flour

1/2 teaspoon baking soda

1/4 teaspoon salt

1/4 teaspoon baking powder

1/2 teaspoon ground cardamom

1/2 cup shredded coconut

1/2 cup granola or 1/4 cup quick rolled oats

3/4 cup chopped pecans

1 1/2 cups semisweet chocolate chips

1 Preheat the oven to 350° F.

2 Cream the shortening and the brown sugar until smooth.

3 Add the egg and vanilla and beat well.

4 Stir in the dates and let the mixture sit for several minutes to soften the dates.

5 Combine the flour, baking soda, salt, baking powder, and cardamom. Sift and set aside.

6 Beat the sugar mixture again until creamy.

7 Slowly add the flour mixture to the sugar mixture and mix well.

8 Stir in the coconut, granola or oats, pecans, and chocolate chips.

9 Drop the batter by the tablespoonful onto a nonstick cookie sheet about 1 1/2 inches apart.

10 Bake 10 to 12 minutes. Remove the cookies immediately to a flat surface to cool. Store in an airtight container.

Easy Double Chocolate Cookies

These use both cocoa and chocolate chips. It's never wrong to use too much of a good thing.

Makes 2 dozen

1/3 cup vegetable shortening

1 cup sugar

2/3 cup brown sugar

3 tablespoons milk

1 tablespoon vanilla

2 eggs

2 cups all-purpose flour

1 cup cocoa

1 teaspoon baking soda

1/2 teaspoon ground cardamom

1/2 teaspoon salt

1 1/2 cups chopped pecans

1 1/2 cups chocolate chips

1 Preheat the oven to 350° F.

2 Cream the shortening, sugar, and brown sugar.

3 Add the milk and vanilla and mix until well blended.

4 Add the eggs one at a time. Beat well after each addition.

5 Combine the flour, cocoa, baking soda, cardamom, and salt. Mix into the sugar mixture.

6 Stir in the nuts and chips.

7 Drop 2 tablespoonfuls of the dough 2 inches apart onto a non-stick cookie sheet.

8 Bake for 10 to 12 minutes and cool for 2 minutes on the cookie sheet. Remove to a flat surface to cool completely.

Chocolate Chip & Peanut
Cookies

This is another cookie that everybody is always asking for, a perfect marriage of chocolate and peanut butter. Double the recipe so you have plenty on hand. These get eaten really fast.

*Makes
2 1/2 dozen*

1/2 cup butter

1/2 cup peanut butter, at room temperature

3/4 cup brown sugar

1/2 cup sugar

2 eggs

1 teaspoon vanilla

1 3/4 cups all-purpose flour

1 teaspoon baking soda

1/2 teaspoon salt

2 cups semisweet chocolate chips

1/2 cup chopped roasted peanuts

1 Preheat the oven to 375° F.

2 Cream the butter, peanut butter, and both sugars until light and fluffy.

3 Beat in the eggs one at a time and add the vanilla.

4 Combine the flour, baking soda, and salt.

5 Blend the two mixtures. Stir in the chips and the peanuts.

6 Drop the batter by the tablespoonful onto a nonstick baking sheet about 1 1/2 inches apart. Flatten slightly with a fork.

7 Bake for 10 to 12 minutes, or until golden brown. Remove from the pan to a flat surface to cool.

Pecan & White Chocolate Chip
Oatmeal Cookies

I put pecans into just about everything, I guess, because of their rich taste. This recipe is worth trying.

*Makes
2 1/2 dozen*

1 cup honey

1/2 cup vegetable shortening

1 egg

1 1/2 cups all-purpose flour, sifted

1/2 teaspoon baking soda

1/2 teaspoon salt

1 1/2 cups quick oats

4 tablespoons sour milk* or buttermilk

2 cups white chocolate chips

1 cup chopped pecans

1 Preheat the oven to 325° F.

2 Cream the honey and the shortening.

3 Add the egg and beat well.

4 Combine the sifted flour with the baking soda, salt, and oats.

5 Combine the buttermilk with the dry ingredients and the egg/honey mixture.

6 Stir in the chips and the pecans.

7 Drop the dough by the tablespoonful onto a nonstick cookie sheet.

8 Bake for 12 to 15 minutes, or until golden.

*Sour milk: Put 2 or 3 drops of lemon juice in 1 cup of milk.

White Chocolate Chip Cookies
with Macadamia Nuts

The white chocolate and Macadamia nuts make this different from most other chocolate chip cookies. I use butter for these, but you can substitute vegetable shortening.

Makes 3 dozen

3/4 cup butter, softened

3/4 cup light brown sugar

3/4 cup sugar

1 teaspoon vanilla

2 eggs

2 cups all-purpose flour

1 teaspoon baking soda

1/2 teaspoon salt

1 package (12 oz.) white chocolate chips

1/3 cup chopped macadamia nuts

1 Preheat the oven to 375° F.

2 Beat the butter, brown sugar, granulated sugar, and vanilla until light and fluffy. Add the eggs and beat well.

3 Mix together the flour, baking soda, and salt.

4 Gradually add the flour mixture to the butter mixture. Mix until the batter is smooth. Stir in the chips and nuts.

5 Drop the batter by the tablespoonful onto a nonstick cookie sheet. Bake the cookies for 8 to 10 minutes.

Basic Sugar Cookies

It's more work to roll out cookie dough, but it's worth it on several counts: one, it's fun to do with children and then decorate the cookies afterward; two, there's a precision in the cookie you sometimes want; three, you can use cookie cutters of various shapes—stars, crescents, spades, clubs, hearts, men, and women. You can ice them with colored frosting and sprinkles.

Makes 3 dozen

2 cups all-purpose flour

1 1/2 teaspoons baking powder

1/2 teaspoon salt

1/2 cup soft butter

1 cup sugar

1 egg

1 teaspoon vanilla

1 tablespoon whipping cream

1 Sift together the flour, baking powder, and salt. Set aside.

2 Cream the butter with the sugar, egg, vanilla, and whipping cream. Mix until smooth and creamy.

3 Stir in the flour mixture. The dough must be stiff enough to roll out. If not, add extra flour, a teaspoon at a time, until it's right.

4 Cover and chill for 2 hours.

5 Preheat the oven to 375° F.

6 Roll the dough out about 1/4-inch thick. Cut out the shapes you want with a cookie cutter.

7 Transfer the cookies to a nonstick cookie sheet and sprinkle with granulated sugar.

8 Bake for 8 to 10 minutes, or until the edges are just turning a light brown. Remove to a flat surface to cool.

Variations

Butterscotch Cookies

Substitute 1 cup brown sugar for the white sugar.

Chocolate Crispy Cookies

Mix and sift 1/2 teaspoon ground cinnamon with the flour. Add 2 oz. melted unsweetened chocolate to the butter-sugar-egg mixture.

Spice Cookies

Mix and sift 1/4 teaspoon each ground cinnamon, ground ginger, ground cloves, and ground allspice with the flour. Omit the vanilla.

Molasses Cookies

The molasses and cinnamon make a difference here.

Makes 3 dozen
2 cups all-purpose flour
1/2 teaspoon baking powder
1/4 teaspoon baking soda
1 teaspoon ground cinnamon
1/2 teaspoon salt
1/2 cup butter
1/2 cup sugar
1/2 cup molasses
1 egg
1 tablespoon whipping cream

1 Sift together the flour, baking powder, baking soda, cinnamon, and salt.

2 Cream together the butter, sugar, and molasses.

3 Beat in the egg and whipping cream.

4 Mix the flour mixture with the sugar mixture.

5 Cover and chill for 2 hours.

6 Preheat the oven to 375° F.

7 Roll the dough out about 1/4-inch thick. Cut the shapes out with a cookie cutter.

8 Transfer the cookies to a nonstick cookie sheet and sprinkle with sugar. Bake for 8 to 10 minutes, or until the edges are just turning a light brown.

Great Grandma's Ginger Cookies

It's important to keep the dough chilled here. Work with small batches at a time, keeping the rest covered with a damp towel in the refrigerator until needed.

*Makes
2 1/2 dozen*

1 cup molasses

1/2 cup butter

2 1/2 cups all-purpose flour

1 tablespoon ground ginger

1/4 teaspoon ground nutmeg

Pinch ground cloves

1/4 teaspoon salt

2 tablespoons baking soda

2 tablespoons warm milk

1 Heat the molasses in a small saucepan to the boiling point.

2 Add the butter to the hot molasses and mix well. When the butter is melted remove from the heat, stir, and let cool.

3 Combine the flour, ginger, nutmeg, cloves, salt, and baking soda.

4 Combine the flour mixture with the molasses mixture. While stirring the two together add the milk.

5 Cover and chill for several hours.

6 Preheat the oven to 350° F.

7 Use 1/4 of the dough at a time, keeping the rest of the dough chilled. Roll out the dough to about a 1/4-inch thickness. Cut the cookies out with a round 2-inch cutter or a glass. Transfer the cookies to a nonstick cookie sheet. Bake for 10 minutes.

Chocolate Cookies

with a White Filling

This is one of my favorite cookies. Don't let the extra steps scare you off. You don't need to roll them out—the dough is refrigerated, and then sliced into rounds.

Makes
1 1/2 dozen

1/2 cup vegetable shortening

1 cup sugar

1 egg

1 teaspoon vanilla

1 cup all-purpose flour

3/4 cup cocoa

3/4 teaspoon baking soda

1/4 teaspoon salt

Filling

1/4 cup butter

3 cups powdered sugar

2 tablespoons milk

1 teaspoon vanilla

1 In a medium bowl, cream the shortening and the sugar.

2 Add the egg and the vanilla and beat until light and fluffy.

3 Sift together the flour, cocoa, baking soda, and salt. Add to the shortening mixture and mix well.

4 Divide the dough in half and shape each part into a 1 1/2-inch thick roll.

5 Wrap each roll in wax paper or plastic wrap and refrigerate 4 or 5 hours.

6 Preheat the oven to 375° F.

7 Cut the dough into 1/4-inch-thick slices.

8   Place the slices about 1 1/2 inches apart on a nonstick cookie sheet and bake for 8 to 10 minutes.

9   Remove the cookies from the cookie sheet to a flat surface to cool.

10 To make the filling, add all the ingredients to a small bowl and beat them until they are spreading consistency. Add more sugar to thicken the filling, more milk to thin it.

11 Spread the filling on the flat side of half the cookies and top with the remaining cookies, forming a sandwich.

Easy and Fast Ginger Snaps

I make sure I have lots of these cookies around when I'm expecting my young friends. For an added touch, I dust them with a little granulated sugar when they first come out of the oven.

Makes
2 1/2 dozen

1 cup molasses

1/2 cup butter

3 1/4 cups all-purpose flour

1/2 teaspoon baking soda

1 tablespoon ground ginger

1/2 teaspoon ground nutmeg

1/4 teaspoon salt

1 In a small saucepan, bring the molasses to the boiling point and stir in the butter.

2 When the butter has melted, take the saucepan off the stove.

3 Mix and sift together the flour, baking soda, ginger, nutmeg, and salt. Add to the molasses and butter mixture and stir until they are blended.

4 Cover and chill for several hours.

5 Preheat the oven to 350° F.

6 Use only 1/4 of the dough at a time, keeping the rest covered with a damp towel and refrigerated. If not, the cookies will come out hard rather then crisp.

7 Roll out the dough about a 1/4-inch thick and cut out with a 2-inch cookie cutter.

8 Transfer the cookies to a nonstick cookie sheet and bake for 10 minutes. Remove them to a flat surface to cool. Then store in an airtight container.

Absolute Best
Cappuccino Brownies

This is my absolute, all-time, favorite brownie recipe. In some ways they taste more like candy than a cake. The espresso and liqueur add the deep taste of coffee to the mix. This is death by chocolate.

3 1/2 tablespoons cocoa

1 1/4 cups all-purpose flour

1/4 teaspoon salt

3/4 cup butter

3 tablespoons canola oil

6 oz. bittersweet chocolate, chopped

1 tablespoon instant espresso

2 cups brown sugar

3 eggs

6 tablespoons coffee liqueur

Frosting

4 oz. cream cheese, softened and whipped

3 tablespoons butter

3/4 cup powdered sugar

1/2 teaspoon vanilla

1/2 teaspoon ground cinnamon

Glaze

4 oz. bittersweet chocolate, chopped

1 tablespoon butter

1/4 cup whipping cream

1 tablespoon instant espresso grains

The Brownies

1 Preheat the oven to 350° F.

2 Grease and flour a 9-inch springform pan.

3 Sift together the cocoa, flour, and salt.

4 Melt the butter, canola oil, and chocolate in a double boiler over low heat, stirring until smooth and creamy. Add the instant espresso and stir.

5 Remove from the heat and let cool for 15 minutes.

6 Add the brown sugar and mix well.

7 Add the eggs one at a time, mixing well after each addition.

8 Add the coffee liqueur.

9 Add the cocoa mixture a third at a time until well incorporated.

10 Spread the batter evenly into the prepared pan.

11 Bake for 30 to 35 minutes. A toothpick should come out clean. Cool completely on a rack.

The Frosting

1 To make the frosting, in a bowl, blend the cream cheese and butter until light and fluffy.

2 Add the sugar, vanilla, and cinnamon. Beat until smooth.

3 Spread the frosting evenly over the cooled brownies. Chill the brownies until set, about 2 hours.

The Glaze

1 To make the glaze, in a double boiler over low heat, melt the chocolate, butter, whipping cream, and espresso. Stir until smooth.

2 Remove from the heat and let cool to room temperature.

3 Spread the glaze evenly over the top of the frosting.

4 Chill the brownies for 3 hours before slicing.

Super Rich Chocolate Brownies

Sometimes there's nothing wrong with overkill: put a square on a dessert plate, a scoop of vanilla ice cream on top, and hot fudge syrup and nuts on top of that.

2 oz. unsweetened chocolate, chopped

3/4 cup semisweet chocolate chips

1/2 cup butter

1 1/3 cups sugar

3 eggs

1 teaspoon vanilla

1 cup all-purpose flour

1/4 teaspoon salt

1 cup chopped walnuts

1 Preheat the oven to 350° F.

2 In the top of a double boiler, melt the two chocolates and butter over hot but not boiling water. Stir until smooth, remove from the heat, and set aside to cool.

3 Beat together the sugar, eggs, and vanilla until smooth.

4 Whisk the sugar mixture into the chocolate mixture.

5 Add the flour and salt. Mix well. Stir in the walnuts.

6 Spread the batter into a greased and floured 9-inch square baking pan and smooth the top with a wooden spoon.

7 Bake for 30 to 40 minutes or until a toothpick inserted into the center of the pan comes out with crumbs adhering to it. Cool the brownies in the pan and then cut into squares.

Espresso Brownies
with a Coffee Liqueur Glaze

These come out moist and dripping with glaze. The espresso adds a rich and smoky flavor.

1/2 cup butter

3 oz. unsweetened chocolate, chopped

2 eggs

1 1/4 cups sugar

2 teaspoons vanilla

3 tablespoons instant espresso grains

3/4 cups all-purpose flour

1/2 teaspoon baking powder

1/4 teaspoon salt

Glaze

8 oz. chocolate chips

3/4 cup butter

1 tablespoon coffee liqueur

The Brownies

1 Preheat the oven to 350° F.

2 Grease and flour a 9-inch baking pan.

3 In a small saucepan or double boiler, melt the butter with the chocolate over low heat. Stir until smooth. Remove the pan from the heat and let it cool.

4 In a bowl, mix together the eggs, sugar, vanilla, and espresso. Beat until thick.

5 Mix in the chocolate mixture and beat until smooth.

6 In another bowl, sift together the flour, baking powder, and salt. Stir into the chocolate mixture and beat until blended well.

7 Spread the batter into the prepared pan and bake in the middle of the oven for 30 minutes, or until a toothpick inserted into the pan comes out clean.

8 Cool the brownies completely on a rack.

The Glaze

1 To make the glaze, melt the chocolate, butter, and liqueur in a double boiler over low heat.

2 Stir until the glaze is smooth and creamy.

3 Cut the brownies into squares and pour the glaze over the top.

4 Chill the brownies until the glaze is set.

Mint Chocolate Brownies

The time-honored mixture of mint and chocolate works gloriously here.

1/2 cup butter

1/4 cup semisweet chocolate chips

1 1/2 cups mint chocolate chips, divided

1 cup sugar

2 eggs

3/4 teaspoon vanilla

2/3 cup all-purpose flour

1/2 teaspoon salt

1/2 cup chopped walnuts

1 Preheat the oven to 350° F.

2 In a double boiler over low heat, melt the butter, chocolate chips, and 1 cup mint chips. Cook and stir until the mixture is smooth and creamy. Cool for 15 minutes and add the sugar. Mix well.

3 Add the eggs one at a time, blending well after each addition. Mix in the vanilla.

4 Combine the flour and salt. Sift the flour into the chocolate mixture and stir. Add the remaining 1/2 cup mint chips and walnuts. Spread the batter evenly into a greased and floured 9-inch baking pan.

5 Bake for 25 to 30 minutes or until a toothpick inserted into the pan comes out clean. Cool the brownies in the pan on a rack before slicing.

Chocolate Chip Pecan Squares

This recipe has just the right touch of chocolate. The pecans add a nice crisp texture.

1/2 cup vegetable shortening

1/2 cup brown sugar

1 egg

1 tablespoon milk

1 teaspoon vanilla

3/4 cup all-purpose flour

1 1/2 cups semisweet chocolate chips, divided

3/4 cup chopped pecans, divided

1 Preheat the oven to 350° F.

2 Cream the shortening and brown sugar until smooth.

3 Add the egg and mix until creamy.

4 Add the milk and vanilla, and mix until well blended.

5 Add the flour and mix until combined. Stir in one cup of the chocolate chips and 1/2 cup of the nuts.

6 Spread the batter evenly into a greased 8-inch square pan. Bake for 25 to 30 minutes or until lightly browned.

7 Remove from the oven. Sprinkle with the rest of the chocolate chips. Wait for a few minutes until the chips have softened, then spread evenly with a knife.

8 Sprinkle with the remaining nuts and cool completely.

Out of This World Spice Bars

This recipe is particularly moist and spicy. I reworked several recipes to come up with one that reminded me of the Fourth of July picnics of my childhood. Don't be afraid to be liberal with the spices.

4 eggs, beaten

1 cup sugar

1/2 cup brown sugar

2 cups whole wheat flour

1/2 teaspoon baking soda

1 teaspoon ground cinnamon

1/2 teaspoon ground cloves

1/4 teaspoon ground nutmeg

1/4 teaspoon ground allspice

1/3 cup raisins

1/3 cup chopped almonds

1 Combine the eggs and both the sugars. Beat until light and creamy.

2 Sift together the flour, baking soda, cinnamon, cloves, nutmeg, and allspice.

3 Gradually beat the flour mixture into the sugar mixture. Add the raisins and the nuts.

4 Refrigerate the batter for at least 3 hours.

5 Roll out the batter to about 1/2-inch thickness. Cut into bars. Remove to a well-greased cookie sheet, cover, and let stand overnight at room temperature.

6 Preheat the oven to 350° F. Bake for 15 minutes. These taste best after they've been stored several days in a covered container.

Oatmeal Chocolate Squares

Dribble a plate with fresh raspberry sauce. Place a square of this on top and garnish it with a few fresh raspberries.

1 1/4 cups rolled oats

1 1/4 cups all-purpose flour

1/2 teaspoon salt

1/2 teaspoon baking soda

1/2 cup vegetable shortening

1 cup brown sugar

2 eggs

1 can (10 oz.) sweetened condensed milk

1/2 cup cocoa

1/2 cup chopped walnuts

2 teaspoons vanilla

1 Preheat the oven to 350° F.

2 Mix together the oats, flour, salt, and baking soda.

3 Cream the shortening and the sugar.

4 Add the eggs one at a time, beating well after each addition.

5 Add the dry ingredients to the sugar mixture and mix well.

6 In a separate bowl, mix together the condensed milk and the cocoa. Stir in the nuts and the vanilla.

7 Spread two-thirds of the oat mixture in the bottom of a nonstick 9-inch square pan. Pour the cocoa mixture on top and drop small spoonfuls of the remaining oat mixture over the top.

8 Bake for 40 to 45 minutes.

Super Easy Shortbread

Shortbread is one of the favorites at Crossing Press. People who don't normally eat dessert will come in and sneak a piece of short-bread when they think no one is looking. All the ingredients should be the same temperature. Don't cut any corners: always use real butter. Make extra dough and freeze it for several months in an air-tight container. It keeps real well.

Makes 2 dozen   **2 cups butter, at room temperature**

1 cup powdered sugar, sifted

4 cups all-purpose flour, sifted

1/2 teaspoon salt

1 Beat the butter until it is light and fluffy. Slowly add the sugar and continue beating until thoroughly blended.

2 Sift together the flour and salt.

3 Add the flour mixture, about 1/4 at a time, to the butter mixture. Continue to mix until the dough is smooth and soft.

4 Working quickly, pat or roll the dough into an even layer about 1/2-inch high. Score the dough into 1 x 2 1/2-inch pieces. With a fork, pierce each piece on top in three places on the diagonal as a design.

5 Transfer the cookies to a nonstick cookie sheet and wrap tightly with plastic wrap.

6 Refrigerate for at least 2 hours to overnight.

7 Preheat the oven to 325° F.

8 Position the racks in the upper third of the oven, reduce the heat to 300° F., and bake for 20 minutes.

9 Turn the cookie sheet around and move it to another part of the oven. Bake for another 14 to 15 minutes.

10 Cool the shortbread on the cookie sheet on a rack for 5 minutes. Remove the shortbread from the cookie sheet to a flat surface to finish cooling.

11 The shortbread can be stored up to a month in an airtight container with wax paper between the layers.

Variations

Hazelnut Shortbread

1 cup chopped toasted hazelnuts

Mix these into the final dough. Any nut will work instead.

Spicy Shortbread

2 teaspoons ground cinnamon

1 teaspoon ground ginger

1/4 teaspoon ground nutmeg

Blend the spices together. As a last step, add the spices to the dough. Continue as directed.

Orange Shortbread

2 teaspoons orange extract

2 tablespoons fresh orange zest

Mix the orange extract in with the butter. After all the flour has been added to the dough, mix in the orange zest. Continue as directed.

Ginger Shortbread

1 tablespoon minced fresh ginger

1 teaspoon ground ginger

After all the flour has been added to the dough, blend in the ginger. Continue as directed.

Easy Butterscotch Bars

Sometimes, nothing satisfies me except butterscotch. This bar blends the flavors of butterscotch and peanut butter perfectly. You don't have to bake these bars. Use lots of peanuts.

Makes 2 dozen

3/8 cup butter, divided

1 package (11 oz.) butterscotch chips

1 cup peanut butter

1/3 cup milk

2 cups graham cracker crumbs

1 cup chopped peanuts

1 1/2 cups semisweet chocolate chips

Finely chopped roasted peanuts, skinless

Dried coconut

1 Combine 1/4 cup of the butter, chips, peanut butter, and milk in top of a double boiler over hot, not boiling, water. Stir until the mixture is melted and smooth.

2 Combine the graham cracker crumbs and peanuts in a large bowl. Combine the two mixtures.

3 Spread the batter in a nonstick 9 x 9 x 2-inch pan and refrigerate until the bars are firm. Cut the dough into bars 1 x 2 inches.

4 Melt the chocolate chips with the remaining 2 tablespoons of butter on top of a double boiler over hot, not boiling, water. Stir until the chocolate is creamy.

5 Place one bar at a time in the melted chocolate, turning with a fork. Lift from the chocolate and allow the excess to drip off. Place the bar on a wax paper lined cookie sheet. Sprinkle with finely chopped nuts and dried coconut.

6 Chill the bars in the refrigerator until they're hard.

Lemon Bars

I have had more discussions about the merits of this or that lemon bar recipe than any other dessert. This is our favorite.

Makes 3 dozen
2 1/4 cups cake flour

1/2 cup powdered sugar

3/4 cup butter

4 eggs

2 cups sugar

1/3 cup lemon juice

1/4 cup all-purpose flour

1 teaspoon baking powder

Powdered sugar, sifted

1 Preheat the oven to 350° F.

2 Combine the cake flour and the powdered sugar. Sift it.

3 In a food processor, blend the butter with the sifted flour until the mixture is crumbly. Press the dough into a greased 9 x 13-inch baking dish.

4 Bake for 15 to 20 minutes or until lightly browned.

5 Meanwhile, beat the eggs, sugar, lemon juice, flour, and baking powder together until smooth and light. Pour the lemon mixture over the partially baked crust.

6 Bake for 30 minutes longer or until the custard is set and golden. Cool on a rack.

7 Before serving, sprinkle with the sifted powdered sugar and cut into 1 x 1 1/2-inch bars.

Macadamia Coconut Bars

These are pretty stacked on a serving tray. Some of my friends feel this is the best bar in the book. You can add either chocolate or butterscotch chips to this recipe, the more the better.

Makes 3 dozen

2 cups all-purpose flour

1 1/4 cups butter, cold and cut into pieces, divided

2/3 cup powdered sugar, sifted

1/2 teaspoon salt

1/2 cup brown sugar

3/4 cup canned coconut cream

1/4 cup whipping cream

3 tablespoons lemon juice

1 cup shredded, sweetened coconut

1 cup macadamia nuts, cut in half

1 Preheat the oven to 350° F.

2 Generously grease a 9 x 13-inch baking dish.

3 In a blender or food processor, mix together the flour, 1 cup of the butter, powdered sugar, and salt. Mix until the ingredients just form a dough. Pat the dough into the bottom of the prepared baking dish. Bake for 20 minutes.

4 In a medium saucepan, melt the remaining 1/4 cup of butter over low heat. Whisk in the brown sugar and cook for 1 minute.

5 Remove from the heat and add the coconut cream, whipping cream, and lemon juice. Mix well. Stir in the coconut and nuts. Pour the mixture over the shortbread.

6 Reduce the oven temperature to 325° F. Bake for 40 to 50 minutes, or until the top is golden and the center is set.

7 Cool completely in the dish set on a rack, then cut into 1 x 1 1/2-inch bars.

Chapter 2

Pies & Cobblers

The success of any pie begins with the crust. It should be delicious and flaky and, most important, easy to work with. When you are using a pie crust with a filling that will be added later, freeze the pie dough for several minutes until it is firm. Line the pie plate with aluminum foil and fill it with dried beans, rice, or weights to ensure it keeps its shape during baking. I have used the foil without anything to weight the crust down, but it doesn't work quite as well.

- Always bake a pie in the lower third of the oven for a crisp bottom crust.
- It's been my experience that sometimes a packaged cake mix is better than a homemade cake, but nothing is as good as a scratch pie crust.
- I use vegetable shortening because I like the flaky texture. I use butter when I need a firmer crust.
- In order to prevent the crust's edge from browning too quickly, cut a 9 x 2-inch-diameter circle from a large square of heavy-duty foil to make a shield. Place it over the crust toward the end of the baking time.
- Let the pie cool so that the filling will firm up. It's easier to cut that way.
- Cooking times for pies are only general guidelines. In double-crusted pies the top should be golden brown with the filling bubbling through the steam vents. The edges of a single-crusted pie should be golden, but not burned. The filling should be set when a toothpick inserted into the center comes out clean.
- Keep a watchful eye on a pie as it bakes, and always preheat the oven beforehand.

Note: The recipes that follow are for a top and bottom crust. If you need only a single crust, either cut the recipe in half or freeze the half you don't use, firmly wrapped in plastic.

Flaky Pie Crust

2 cups all-purpose flour
2 teaspoons sugar
3/4 teaspoon salt
1 cup butter flavored vegetable shortening, chilled
4 tablespoons ice cold water

1 Sift together the flour, sugar, and salt.

2 Cut the shortening into the flour. I usually do this in a food processor set on pulse. But you can also do it by hand with two knives. Blend until the mixture resembles large peas and is fairly uniform. Do not overmix.

3 Sprinkle the water over the dough one tablespoon at a time. Lightly mix with a fork between each spoonful of water. Don't overwork the dough, but get it to the point where it holds together.

4 Turn the dough out onto a floured surface and form it into a firm ball with a minimum of handling. Wrap the dough in plastic wrap and refrigerate for 30 minutes.

5 Take half the dough and roll out to about 1/8-inch thickness. Place it on the bottom of a greased pie plate.

6 If the recipe calls for a top crust, roll out the other half of the dough. Fill the pie plate with whatever you wish, and cover the filling with the dough. Crimp the edges together.

7 Cut steam holes in the top and bake according to the recipe instructions.

Pie Crust

2 1/4 cups all-purpose flour

1/2 teaspoon salt

3/4 cup butter, chilled

5 to 7 tablespoons ice cold water

1 Sift together the flour and salt.

2 Cut the butter into the flour. I usually do this in a food processor set on pulse. But you can also do it by hand with two knives. Blend until the mixture resembles large peas and is fairly uniform.

3 Sprinkle the water over the dough one tablespoon at a time. Lightly mix with a fork between each spoonful of water. Don't overwork the dough, but get it to the point where it holds together.

4 Turn the dough out onto a floured surface and form it into a firm ball with a minimum of handling. Wrap the dough in plastic wrap and refrigerate for 30 minutes.

5 Divide the dough in half and roll out each half to about 1/8-inch thickness.

6 With one half, line the bottom of a greased pie plate.

7 If the recipe calls for a top crust, drape the other rolled out round over the top of the filled pie and crimp the edges together.

8 Cut steam holes in the top and bake according to the recipe instructions.

Whole Wheat Pie Crust

1 3/4 cups all-purpose flour

2/3 cup whole wheat pastry flour

1/4 teaspoon salt

5 tablespoons butter, cold

5 tablespoons vegetable shortening, chilled

7 to 8 tablespoons ice cold water

1 Sift together the flours and salt.

2 Cut the butter and shortening into the flour. I usually do this in a food processor set on pulse. But you can also do it by hand with two knives. Blend until the mixture resembles large peas and is fairly uniform. Do not overmix.

3 Sprinkle the water over the dough one tablespoon at a time. Lightly mix with a fork between each spoonful of water. Don't overwork the dough, but get it to the point where it holds together.

4 Turn the dough out onto a floured surface and form it into a firm ball with a minimum of handling. Wrap the dough in plastic wrap and refrigerate for 30 minutes.

5 Cut the dough in half and roll out each half to about 1/8-inch thickness.

6 With one half, line the bottom of a greased pie plate.

7 If the recipe calls for a top crust, drape the other rolled out round over the top of the filled pie and crimp the edges together.

8 Cut steam holes in the top and bake according to the recipe instructions.

Vinegar Pie

I had heard about vinegar pie for years, but no one I knew in California seemed to know about it. I searched the cookbooks and couldn't find a recipe for it anywhere. When my friend Ray moved to the South, I asked him if he could help me out. Here's the recipe he found. It's really great, like a tart pumpkin pie.

Single pie crust **5 eggs, at room temperature**

2 tablespoons all-purpose flour

1 cup sugar

1/4 cup butter, melted and cooled

3 tablespoons cider vinegar

1 teaspoon vanilla

1/2 cup raisins

1/2 teaspoon ground cinnamon

1/4 teaspoon ground nutmeg

1 cup sour cream

1 Preheat the oven to 300° F.

2 Prepare a single pastry crust.

3 Beat the eggs in a large bowl.

4 Add the flour, sugar, butter, vinegar, vanilla, raisins, cinnamon, nutmeg, and sour cream. Stir until just mixed.

5 Add the filling to the pie pan.

6 Bake for 1 hour or until the top is golden and the filling is set.

7 Serve warm or chilled.

Classic American Apple Pie

Flags, fireworks, picnics, and apple pie—this is the one that takes all the ribbons at the state fair, the one you will see at all the family reunions and church socials.

Double pie crust **1 egg, slightly beaten**

1/4 cup water

8 cups sliced, peeled apples

1 cup sugar

1 teaspoon ground cinnamon

1/4 teaspoon ground nutmeg

2 tablespoons cornstarch

2 teaspoons fresh lemon juice

1 teaspoon fresh lemon zest

2 tablespoons butter, cut into pieces

1 Preheat the oven to 425° F.

2 Divide the pastry dough in half and roll out into two 1/4-inch rounds.

3 Combine the egg with the water.

4 Line a 9-inch pie plate with one round and brush the bottom with about half of the egg wash. This will seal the dough.

5 In a large bowl, combine the apples, sugar, cinnamon, nutmeg, and cornstarch. Allow this mixture to stand for 20 minutes.

6 Mix in the lemon juice and zest.

7 Arrange the apple slices in the pie shell in flat, snug layers. Build up a higher mound of apples in the center because the apples will cook down as they bake.

8 Pour the juices from the bowl over the apples and dot with the butter.

9 Ease the top crust in place. Seal and crimp the edges, and slit the top in several places to vent the steam.

10 Brush the top crust with the remaining egg wash.

11 Bake for 15 minutes. Lower the oven to 400° F and continue baking for about 40 minutes or until the crust is golden.

12 For a sugared crust, brush the pie again with any leftover egg wash 5 minutes before the pie is done. Sprinkle with sugar and continue baking.

Dutch Apple Raisin Pie

Choose the ripest, sweetest apples, free from blemishes. The brandy makes this pie exceptional.

Double pie crust **2 cups golden raisins**

1/2 cup water

1/2 cup brandy

1/2 cup plus 2 tablespoons sugar, divided

1 tablespoon cornstarch

1 teaspoon ground cinnamon

1/4 teaspoon salt

1 tablespoon fresh lemon juice

4 cups sliced, peeled apples

1 egg, beaten

1 Preheat the oven to 425° F.

2 In a small saucepan over low heat, simmer the raisins in the water and brandy until most of the liquid is absorbed. Mix 1/2 cup of the sugar, cornstarch, cinnamon, and salt. Stir this into the raisin mixture along with the lemon juice and apples.

3 Divide the pie crust dough in half and roll out two rounds. Line a 9-inch pie plate with one round.

4 Fill the pie plate with the apple mixture and cover with the other round. Seal and flute the edges. Cut several slits in the top for steam vents and brush with the beaten egg. Sprinkle evenly with the remaining 2 tablespoons of sugar.

5 Bake for 10 minutes, then reduce the heat to 350° F. Bake for 45 to 55 minutes or until the crust is golden.

Pineapple-Glazed Apple Pie

This is a great no-bake apple pie. If the apples are ripe and juicy you can cut back on some of the sugar if you like.

Single pie crust **1 3/4 cups pineapple juice, divided**

1 cup sugar

10 sliced, peeled apples

3 tablespoons cornstarch

1 tablespoon butter

1 teaspoon vanilla

1/4 teaspoon salt

1 Preheat the oven to 400° F.

2 Prepare the pie crust and line a 9-inch glass pie plate. Line with foil and pie weights. Bake for 10 or 15 minutes, or until the crust is just turning golden.

3 In a large saucepan, combine 1 1/2 cups of the pineapple juice with the sugar. Bring to a light boil over medium heat. Add the apples. Simmer for 3 or 4 minutes until the apples are tender but not soft. With a slotted spoon remove the apples and set aside.

4 Mix the cornstarch into the remaining 1/4 cup of pineapple juice and add it to the boiling liquid in the saucepan. Cook and stir until the mixture thickens and bubbles, then cook for a couple of minutes more. Remove the saucepan from the heat and stir in the butter, vanilla, and salt. Reduce the heat to low. Cover and cook for at least 30 minutes without stirring.

5 Pour half the pineapple mixture into the pie shell spreading it to cover the bottom. Arrange the apples on top and pour the remaining mixture over the top. Cover and refrigerate until chilled and set.

Mock Mince Pie

If you're looking for a vegetarian alternative to this holiday classic, here it is. Some of my friends like it even better than its famous cousin. It's good served with whipped cream. Sometimes my friends put a bit of dark rum into the whipped cream.

Double pie crust **3 pounds peeled, chopped apples**

1/2 cup pitted, chopped prunes

1/2 cup golden raisins

1/2 cup brown sugar

1/4 cup molasses

1/4 cup brandy

1/4 cup fresh orange juice

1/4 cup butter, cut in pieces

2 tablespoons dark rum

1 tablespoon orange zest

1 teaspoon lemon zest

1 teaspoon ground cinnamon

1/4 teaspoon ground cloves

1/4 teaspoon allspice

1/4 teaspoon ground nutmeg

1/4 teaspoon salt

1 egg white, beaten

1 Prepare the pie crust.

2 Divide the dough in half and roll out two 13-inch rounds. Fit one into a 9-inch pie plate and flute the edge. Cover and refrigerate both the unused round and the lined pie plate.

3 Combine all the other ingredients in a large heavy-bottomed saucepan and cook over low heat for about 1 1/2 hours or until the apples are tender and the mixture is thick. Stir occasionally.

4 Cool the filling completely.

5 Preheat the oven to 400° F.

6 Spoon the filling into the dough-covered pie plate, gently pressing the filling flat.

7 Cover the top with the second round and crimp the edges with a fork. Slash several slits in the top for steam vents and brush the top of the pie dough with the egg whites.

8 Bake for about 40 minutes or until the top of the pie is a golden brown and the mince is bubbling. Cool completely before serving.

Pear, Ginger, &

Golden Raisin Pie

When you start seeing Bartlett or Anjou pears in the stores, that's the time to make this pie. I've tried the same recipe with canned pears, but decided fresh is the only way to go.

Double pie crust **1 cup golden raisins**

2 tablespoons grated fresh ginger

1/4 cup brandy

3 pounds ripe pears, peeled, cored, and sliced thin

1/2 cup plus 1 tablespoon sugar, divided

1/4 cup butter, melted

2 tablespoons instant tapioca

1 tablespoon fresh lemon juice

1 teaspoon ground cinnamon

1/4 teaspoon ground nutmeg

1 egg, beaten

1 Prepare the pie dough. Roll out two 13-inch rounds and line a 9-inch pie plate with one of the rounds. Refrigerate both the unused round and the lined pie plate.

2 Combine the raisins, ginger, and brandy in a heavy saucepan. Add enough water to just cover. Simmer over low heat until the liquid is absorbed.

3 Cool completely.

4 Preheat the oven to 400° F.

5 Combine the pears, 1/2 cup sugar, butter, tapioca, lemon juice, and the spices in a large bowl.

6 Stir in the raisin mixture.

7 Spoon the pear mixture into the pie plate, mounding in the center.

8 Ease the other round over the top of the pears. Crimp the edges together with a fork and cut slits in the top for steam vents.

9 Bake for 45 minutes.

10 Brush the beaten egg on the top crust. Sprinkle the remaining tablespoon of sugar over the top.

11 Bake for 10 to 15 minutes longer or until the crust is golden brown and the juices are bubbling up through the steam vents.

12 Serve warm.

Pear Pie with
Ginger, Pepper, & Lemon

Pears and ginger were made for each other. Don't be afraid of the pepper in this recipe. Try to think of it as an adventure.

Single pie crust

Topping

1/4 cup chilled butter, cut into pieces

1/2 cup sugar

1/4 cup all-purpose flour

Filling

3 pounds ripe pears, peeled, cored, and sliced thin

1/2 cup golden raisins

1/2 cup sugar

1/4 cup all-purpose flour

1 tablespoon fresh lemon zest

1 tablespoon grated fresh ginger

1 teaspoon fresh ground pepper

1 To make the topping, add the butter to the sugar and flour, and mix until the dough is the size of small peas. Cover and refrigerate the mixture until you are ready to use it.

2 Preheat the oven to 450° F.

3 Combine all the ingredients for the filling and mix well. Spoon the filling into the prepared pie crust. Sprinkle the topping evenly over the top.

4 Place the pie on a baking sheet lined with foil and bake for 10 minutes. Reduce the heat to 350° F and bake for 1 hour more.

Deep Dish Peach Pie

The peaches and raisins are an interesting combination here. I like this best with a crumb topping. Simply break up 25 or 30 cinnamon graham crackers in the food processor and pulse until they are coarsely chopped. Pulse in 2 tablespoons of melted butter until all the crumbs are moist. Sprinkle over the top of the fruit and bake.

Double pie crust **12 cups peeled, sliced peaches**

1/2 cup golden raisins

1 1/4 cups sugar

1/3 cup cornstarch

1/2 teaspoon ground cinnamon

1/4 teaspoon ground nutmeg

1/4 teaspoon salt

3 tablespoons butter

1 Preheat the oven to 425° F.

2 Combine the peaches and raisins in a large bowl.

3 In another bowl, combine the sugar, cornstarch, cinnamon, nutmeg, and salt.

4 Combine the two mixtures carefully.

5 Fill a greased 9 x 13-inch baking dish with the fruit mixture. Dot the fruit with the butter.

6 Roll out the pastry dough to fit over the baking dish. Place the pastry on top of the fruit and secure to the sides by crimping the dough to the dish. Cut several vent holes in the pastry.

7 Bake for 15 minutes. Reduce the heat to 325° F. and bake for an additional 40 to 50 minutes or until the crust is golden. Remove from the oven and let the pie sit for 15 or 20 minutes before serving.

Ginger Peach Pie

There's nothing I like better than a peach pie in the middle of sum-mer when the peaches are at their finest. To skin the peaches easi-ly, dunk them in a pot of boiling water for 2 to 3 minutes. Cool them in a pot of cold water, drain, and with hardly any rubbing the skin should slide right off. The ginger makes this recipe especially inter-esting.

Double pie crust **1 tablespoon fresh lemon juice**

2 tablespoons minced fresh ginger

1 teaspoon ground cinnamon

2/3 cup plus 1 tablespoon sugar, divided

1/4 cup instant tapioca

3 1/2 pounds fresh peaches

1 egg white, slightly beaten, divided

2 1/2 tablespoons butter

1 Preheat the oven to 425° F.

2 In a large bowl, combine the lemon juice, ginger, cinnamon, 2/3 cup sugar, and tapioca.

3 Peel the peaches and cut into thick slices. Toss the peach slices with the lemon juice mixture.

4 Divide the dough in half, and roll out two large rounds, about 1/8-inch thick and large enough to fit a lightly greased 9-inch pie tin. Use one round to cover the bottom of the pie tin.

5 With a pastry brush, paint the bottom dough with half of the egg white. This will seal it.

6 Add the peach filling. Cut the butter into pieces and arrange around the top of the peaches.

7 Drape the second round on top, crimp the edges, and slash the top in several places to make steam vents.

8 Bake for 15 minutes, reduce the heat to 400° F., and bake for 40 more minutes.

9 Brush the top with the remaining egg white and sprinkle with the remaining tablespoon of sugar. Bake for 5 more minutes or until the top is golden. Serve this pie warm or at room temperature.

Brandied Fruit Pie

This is so good I make it even in the summertime when fresh fruit is available.

Single pie crust **2 packages (8-oz. each) mixed dried fruit**

1 cup water

1/4 cup brandy, or 1 tablespoon brandy extract

1 lemon, sliced thin

3/4 cup brown sugar

1 teaspoon ground cinnamon

1/4 teaspoon ground nutmeg

1/4 teaspoon ground cloves

1/4 teaspoon salt

1 Preheat the oven to 350° F.

2 In a medium saucepan, combine the dried fruit, water, brandy or brandy extract, and lemon slices. Simmer over low heat until most of the liquid is absorbed, about 10 minutes. Remove and discard the lemon slices. Stir in the sugar, spices, and salt. Set aside for about 30 minutes to cool.

3 Pour the fruit mixture into the prepared pie crust and sprinkle graham cracker crumbs over the top. (See page 59 for directions.)

4 Bake for 30 minutes and cool on a rack. Serve warm or at room temperature.

Sweet Potato Spice Pie

This is a recipe my friend Ray sent me from Louisiana. I've found sweet potatoes are better here than yams.

Single pie crust   **2 pounds sweet potatoes**

1 cup brown sugar

3 eggs

1/4 teaspoon salt

1/2 teaspoon ground cinnamon

1/2 teaspoon ground nutmeg

1/2 teaspoon ground ginger

1/2 teaspoon ground cloves

1/4 teaspoon ground allspice

1/4 teaspoon ground cardamom

1/4 teaspoon ground coriander

1/2 cup whipping cream

1/2 cup half-and-half

3 tablespoons bourbon, or 1 tablespoon brandy extract

1 tablespoon vanilla

1 Preheat the oven to 400° F. Bake the sweet potatoes on a small baking sheet lined with foil for about 1 hour. Cool, peel, and mash with a fork in a large bowl.

2 Bake the crust. Line the crust gently with aluminum foil and fill with pie weights. Bake for about 15 to 20 minutes, or until golden.

3 To the mashed sweet potatoes, add the remaining ingredients. Mix well. Pour into the baked pie crust. Bake for 10 minutes and reduce the heat to 350° F. Finish baking for 40 minutes, or until the filling is set in the middle. Serve warm or at room temperature.

Sweet Potato Pecan Pie

*This is one of my great grandma's recipes. She gave it to her daugh-
ter, my grandma, who then gave it to me when I started cooking
professionally. Use sweet potatoes instead of yams for best results.
If you have extra pecans, throw them in. Her philosophy was "more
is better."*

Single pie crust **2 pounds sweet potatoes**

1/2 cup brown sugar

2 tablespoons maple syrup

1 egg

1 tablespoon whipping cream

1 tablespoon butter, soft

1 tablespoon vanilla

1/4 teaspoon salt

1/4 teaspoon ground cinnamon

1/4 teaspoon ground allspice

1/4 teaspoon ground nutmeg

4 eggs

1 cup sugar

1/2 cup maple syrup

1/2 cup corn syrup

1/4 cup butter, melted

2 cups pecans, halved

1 Preheat the oven to 400° F.

2 On a small baking sheet, bake the sweet potatoes for about 1
hour or until they are done.

3 Line a pie plate with the dough. Gently cover the dough with
aluminum foil and fill with pie weights. Bake in the same 400°
F. oven after the sweet potatoes come out.

4 When the potatoes have cooled, peel them and mash them with a fork.

5 Add all the ingredients except the syrup topping and beat until smooth, but do not overbeat.

6 To make the topping, in a medium bowl, whisk the eggs, sugar, maple syrup, and corn syrup until the mixture is smooth. Whisk in the melted butter.

7 Reduce the oven heat to 350° F.

8 Fill the pie crust with the sweet potato mixture.

9 Arrange the pecan halves on top. Gently ladle the syrup topping over the nuts.

10 Bake for about 50 minutes or until the top is set and puffy.

11 Cool to room temperature and serve.

Karen's Classic Pecan Pie

My friend Karen Narita bakes a pecan pie that is far better than mine. Whenever we have a party or special something going on, Karen is always asked to bring her pies. She was kind enough to give me her recipe for this book. This is something special!

Single pie crust   **4 eggs**
2/3 cup dark corn syrup
2/3 cup light corn syrup
1/3 cup sugar
1 1/2 tablespoons all-purpose flour
1 1/2 teaspoons vanilla
1 1/3 cups chopped pecans
8 pecan halves

1 Preheat the oven to 350° F.

2 Combine the eggs, corn syrups, sugar, flour, and vanilla in a bowl. Beat until well blended.

3 Add the chopped pecans and pour into the pie shell.

4 Lay the pecan halves on top to garnish.

5 Bake for 45 minutes or until the center of the pie rises slightly and is a light brown.

6 Serve at room temperature or chilled.

Chocolate Chunk Pecan Pie

This is one of my favorites. The blend of chocolate and pecans is a match made in dessert heaven.

Single pie crust   **2 cups pecans, toasted**

1 cup chopped semisweet chocolate

3 tablespoons all-purpose flour

3/4 cup softened butter

1 cup brown sugar

5 eggs

1 cup light corn syrup

2 tablespoons molasses

2 teaspoons vanilla

1/2 teaspoon salt

1 Preheat the oven to 400° F. Bake the pie crust until the sides are set, about 10 minutes. Pierce the bottom of the dough with a fork. Bake for another 4 minutes or until the edges are golden. Let it cool. Reduce the oven temperature to 350° F.

2 Mix the pecans, chocolate, and flour in a bowl and set aside.

3 Cream the butter and sugar until light and fluffy. Add the eggs one at a time. Mix well. Add the corn syrup, molasses, vanilla, and salt.

4 Sprinkle the pecans and chocolate on the bottom of the pie shell until it is evenly distributed. Pour the sugar mixture over the top.

5 Bake for 35 or 40 minutes or until the filling is set. Cool before serving.

Texas Pecan Pie

My good friend Ray and his wife moved to Louisiana to start a bed and breakfast in an old planter's mansion they have restored. We've worked in kitchens together off and on for years, so I asked him to send me any southern recipes that he liked a lot.

Single pie crust **1 egg, beaten**

3 oz. bittersweet chocolate, chopped

1 1/2 cups pecans, halved

1 cup brown sugar

3/4 cup light corn syrup

2 tablespoons bourbon, or 1 teaspoon brandy extract

2 teaspoons vanilla

5 eggs

1/3 cup plus 1 tablespoon butter, melted and cooled

1 Preheat the oven to 425° F.

2 Bake the crust for 10 minutes or until it begins to brown.

3 Brush the crust with the beaten egg and bake 5 minutes longer, or until the egg wash is dry and set.

4 Sprinkle the chocolate over the hot crust and let it soften.

5 Spread the chocolate over the inside of the crust.

6 Refrigerate the crust until the chocolate is set, about 15 minutes.

7 Sprinkle the pecans evenly over the chocolate.

8 Beat the sugar, corn syrup, bourbon, and vanilla together until smooth.

9 Add the eggs one at a time. Beat to blend after each addition.

10 Mix in the butter.

11 Pour the filling into the crust.

12 Bake for 55 minutes or until the center of the pie is loosely set and the top is brown.

13 Watch the pie carefully at this point and cover the edges with aluminum foil if they are getting dark.

14 Cool before serving.

Crustless Coconut Pecan Pie

For a nuttier taste, roast the coconut before mixing it in the batter.

1 1/2 cups milk

1 cup sugar

1 cup shredded, unsweetened coconut

3/4 cup all-purpose flour

4 eggs, at room temperature

1 cup chopped pecans

1/4 cup butter, softened

1 1/2 teaspoons vanilla

3/4 teaspoon baking powder

1/4 teaspoon salt

Toasted coconut

1 Preheat the oven to 325° F.

2 Grease a 10-inch pie pan.

3 Add all the ingredients except the toasted coconut to a food processor or blender. Pulse until well blended.

4 Pour the mixture into the prepared pan.

5 Bake for 35 minutes or until golden brown and the center is firm to the touch.

6 Serve warm, garnished with toasted coconut on top.

Mile High Pie

This lemon pie is good to eat and pretty to look at. I use lots of egg whites and really pile on the meringue. I got the recipe from a restaurant I worked at many years ago.

Single pie crust **2 cups sugar, divided**

6 tablespoons cornstarch

1/2 cup fresh lemon juice

8 eggs, separated

1 1/2 cups boiling water

2 tablespoons butter

1/2 teaspoon cream of tartar

1 Preheat the oven to 400° F. Bake a single crust until it's the right color. Remove the crust from the oven. Reduce the oven temperature to 350° F.

2 In a heavy saucepan, combine 1 1/3 cups sugar and the cornstarch. Mix in the lemon juice. Beat 4 egg yolks until light and lemon color and add to the sugar mixture. Store the other 4 egg yolks for another use. Over medium heat, gradually add the water, stirring constantly. Stir until the mixture boils and thickens, about 10 minutes. Remove from the heat and add the butter. Stir until melted. Pour into the pie shell.

3 In a medium bowl, beat the egg whites with the cream of tartar until soft peaks form, and gradually add the remaining 2/3 cup of sugar. Beat until stiff but not dry. Pile the meringue on top of the pie, sealing the meringue carefully to the edge of the shell.

4 Bake 12 to 15 minutes or until the meringue is golden brown. Cool to room temperature before serving.

Chocolate Mousse Pie

This recipe goes together fast. The crust is baked, but the pie is not.

3 cups ground chocolate cookie crumbs

1/4 cup butter, at room temperature

1/2 cup finely chopped semisweet chocolate

1 tablespoon vanilla

Pinch salt

3 cups whipping cream, divided

1/2 cup powdered sugar

1 Preheat the oven to 350° F. Grease a 9-inch springform pan.

2 Put the cookie crumbs and the butter in a processor and blend until the mixture is evenly moistened. Press the crumbs onto the bottom and up the sides of the pan to form a thin crust. Wash the processor. Bake the crust for 5 minutes and transfer to a rack to cool.

3 Put the chocolate, vanilla, and salt in the processor.

4 Add 1 cup of the cream to a small saucepan over low heat and bring it nearly to a boil. Gradually pour the hot cream through the feeder tube of the processor with the machine running and process until the chocolate is melted and smooth. Cool to room temperature, pulsing occasionally.

5 Whip the remaining cream and gradually add the sugar until stiff peaks are formed. Fold into the chocolate mixture. Pour the mousse into the prepared crust. Chill until set, about 5 hours to overnight. Serve with additional whipped cream.

Berry Pie

When I was a little boy we had several rows of boysenberries grow-ing in our backyard. So from the first of July to about the end of September there was always a berry pie in the pantry.

Double pie crust **1 egg white, beaten, divided**

4 cups fresh berries

1 cup plus 1 tablespoon sugar, divided

2 teaspoons fresh lemon juice

1 tablespoon cornstarch

1/3 cup all-purpose flour

2 tablespoons butter, cut in pieces

1 Preheat the oven to 350° F. Line a pie plate with half the pas-try crust. Brush the inside of the dough with part of the egg white to seal it.

2 Combine the berries, 1 cup of the sugar, and lemon juice in a large bowl. Let it sit for at least 15 minutes.

3 Mix the cornstarch with the flour and gently mix into the berries. Pour the berries into the pie plate and dot with the butter.

4 Roll out the remaining dough round and cut it into 1/2-inch-wide strips. Weave the dough strips on top of the filling in a lattice pattern, pinching the edges to seal.

5 Bake for about 1 hour, or until the lattice is light brown. Brush the lattice with the remaining egg white and sprinkle with one tablespoon of sugar. Continue baking until it becomes golden brown, about 10 minutes. Cool before serving.

Light Pumpkin Pie

This recipe retains all the integrity of the original without the extra calories. It's a great dessert after a big holiday meal. This recipe will make two pies. One can be frozen for up to two months, defrosted, and then baked.

Single pie crust **6 egg whites, beaten**

1 can (29-oz.) unsweetened pumpkin

1 cup sugar

2 teaspoons ground cinnamon

1 teaspoon ground ginger

1/2 teaspoon ground cloves

3 cups evaporated skim milk

1 Preheat the oven to 400° F.

2 Prepare the pie crust.

3 Roll out in two 13-inch rounds and line two 9-inch pie plates. Line with aluminum foil and fill with pie weights.

4 Bake for 15 minutes or until the crust is turning golden.

5 Increase the oven heat to 425° F.

6 Combine all the other ingredients in a large bowl and beat until smooth.

7 Pour the filling into the pie crust.

8 Bake for 15 minutes. Reduce the heat to 350° F. and bake for about 40 minutes longer or until a knife inserted in the middle comes out clean. Cool on a rack.

Amaretto Pumpkin Pie

I like standard recipes that have a twist to them, in this case Amaretto.

Single pie crust   **1/4 cup Amaretti cookie crumbs**

2 cups unsweetened canned pumpkin

1 1/3 cups milk

1/2 cup brown sugar

2 tablespoons all-purpose flour

3 tablespoons Amaretto

1 1/2 teaspoons ground cinnamon

1/4 teaspoon ground ginger

1 1/2 teaspoons vanilla

1/2 teaspoon almond extract

2 eggs, beaten

1 Preheat the oven to 400° F.

2 Prepare the pie crust and line a 9-inch glass pie dish. Crimp the edges tightly to the edge of the pie plate to keep the dough from falling in on itself.

3 Spread the Amaretti cookie crumbs evenly across the bottom of the pie plate.

4 Reduce the heat to 375° F. and bake for 10 minutes.

5 Combine the pumpkin and the remaining ingredients in a large bowl and whisk until smooth.

6 Pour the mixture into the baked crust.

7 Bake for 45 minutes or until a knife inserted in the center comes out clean.

8 Serve at room temperature or chilled.

Boysenberry Cobbler

This is very easy to put together.

3 tablespoons cornstarch

3 tablespoons water

1/2 cup unsweetened boysenberry syrup

1/2 teaspoon cinnamon

1 cup all-purpose flour

1 1/2 teaspoons baking powder

1/2 teaspoon salt

2 tablespoons melted butter

1/4 cup boysenberry yogurt

3 cups boysenberries

1/4 cup sugar

1 Preheat the oven to 400° F. Grease a 9 x 13-inch baking dish.

2 Stir the cornstarch into the water until it dissolves. Mix in the syrup and cinnamon. Set aside.

3 Sift together the flour, baking powder, and salt.

4 In a separate bowl, combine the butter and yogurt. Stir in the flour mixture and mix gently with a fork until just combined. Knead the dough 20 or 30 seconds. On a floured surface, roll out the dough to approximately a 1/4 to 1/2-inch thickness and wide enough to cover the baking dish.

5 Mix the berries, yogurt mixture, and sugar. Combine with the syrup mixture.

6 Pour the berry filling into the baking dish and ease the dough into place over the top. Press the dough against the sides of the dish and cut slits for air vents.

7 Turn the oven down to 375° F. and bake for 20 to 25 minutes, or until the crust is a light brown. Serve warm.

Blackberry/Peach Crisp

This juicy and highly flavored crisp becomes thicker upon cooling. The combination of berries and peaches is great. Note that the topping contains oats.

1 cup rolled oats

1 cup packed brown sugar

3/4 cup all-purpose flour, divided

1/2 cup butter

6 cups blackberries

4 cups peeled, sliced peaches

1 Preheat the oven to 350° F.

2 Combine the oats, brown sugar, and 1/2 cup flour in the food processor. Pulse 3 or 4 times to mix the ingredients.

3 Add the butter and pulse until well blended and moist enough to form a ball. Set aside.

4 Toss the berries with the remaining 1/4 cup flour.

5 Add the peaches and stir gently.

6 Pour the fruit into a 9 x 13-inch baking dish.

7 Break up the crumb mixture and sprinkle evenly over the fruit.

8 Bake for 35 to 40 minutes or until the topping is a golden brown.

9 Serve warm.

Fast Cherry Cobbler

Cobblers are fast to make, and this is the fastest of all. Let this cobbler cool slightly and then serve it.

Double pie crust **4 (16 1/2-oz.) cans pitted sweet cherries, drained**

1 cup sugar

1/4 cup all-purpose flour

1 Preheat the oven to 450° F.

2 Combine the cherries, sugar, and flour in a mixing bowl. Toss to coat the cherries and transfer to a 9 x 13-inch baking dish.

3 Roll out the dough and place on top of the cherries. Crimp the edges and cut several slits for steam vents.

4 Bake for 15 to 20 minutes or until the crust is light brown and the filling is bubbly.

Peach/Apple Crisp

The minute the topping on this crust is done pull it from the oven and let it cool. I like the difference between the texture of the peaches and apples.

3 cups peeled, sliced peaches

2 cups peeled, sliced apples

1/4 cup honey

1 teaspoon brandy extract

1/2 teaspoon vanilla

1/4 teaspoon ground cinnamon

Topping

1/2 cup all-purpose flour

1/4 cup rolled oats

1/2 cup brown sugar

4 tablespoons butter

2 tablespoons toasted pine nuts

1 Preheat the oven to 375° F.

2 Combine the peaches, apples, honey, brandy extract, vanilla, and cinnamon in a large bowl. Toss well to coat.

3 Transfer the mixture to a greased 9 x 13-inch baking dish and set aside.

4 Combine the flour, oats, and brown sugar in a bowl.

5 Put the mixture into a processor, add the butter, and pulse until the mixture resembles coarse meal.

6 Stir in the pine nuts.

7 Sprinkle the flour mixture evenly over the peach mixture.

8 Bake for 30 minutes or until lightly browned and bubbly.

9 Serve warm.

Fast Peach Cobbler

Here's another quick cobbler recipe.

12 cups peeled, sliced peaches

1 1/2 cups sugar

1/4 cup instant tapioca

1 tablespoon fresh lemon juice

3 teaspoons lemon zest

1/2 teaspoon ground cinnamon

1/4 teaspoon ground nutmeg

1/4 teaspoon salt

1 package refrigerated biscuit dough

1 Preheat the oven to 425° F. Position the rack in the lowest third of the oven.

2 Place the peaches in a large bowl and add the sugar, tapioca, lemon juice, lemon zest, cinnamon, nutmeg, and salt. Toss until the peaches are well coated with the spices and let them stand for about 10 minutes.

3 Transfer the peaches to a greased 9 x 13-inch baking dish.

4 Top the mixture with the biscuit rounds, spacing them evenly.

5 Bake for almost an hour or until the biscuits are a deep golden brown and the juices are bubbly and thick.

Chapter 3

Cakes, Frostings, & Fillings

Throughout our culture, cake plays a central role in all types of celebrations, from the humble cupcake with one candle on it, to the elaborately trimmed multi-tiered wedding cake. There is no substitute for the joy and taste of a cake baked in your kitchen from raw ingredients. For me, when a cake comes out of the oven, big, full, and steaming, it's the closest I can get to real magic.

- Always bake a cake, no matter what type it is, in a preheated oven, and put it in that preheated oven as soon as it is mixed. The leavening agents begin to work even before a cake is baked, but they need the heat of the oven to finish their work. They will start to lose some of their power if you wait too long.
- Don't open the oven door during the first half of the baking process. A cake can fall if the temperature varies during this time.
- A cake is done when the center springs back when touched with a finger, or when a tester comes out of the center clean.
- Cake freezes well and will keep for several months. Freeze the cake unfrosted and unfilled.
- Allow the cake to cool to room temperature and wrap it in plastic wrap or aluminum foil before freezing.

I've tried to develop easy frostings and fillings to cut down the time spent in the kitchen. These recipes are foolproof. You can lighten most of them if you wish by using margarine instead of butter, or using low-fat sour cream. You will get pretty much the same results. Most of the frostings can also be used as fillings.

Easy & Fast Chocolate Cake

This is one of those foolproof recipes where this sheet cake almost bakes itself. It can be iced with any of your favorite frostings.

1/2 cup cocoa

1/2 cup boiling water

1 cup vegetable shortening

2 cups sugar

1 teaspoon vanilla

2 eggs

2 1/4 cups all-purpose flour

1 1/2 teaspoons baking soda

1/4 teaspoon salt

1 1/3 cups buttermilk

1 Preheat the oven to 350° F.

2 Stir the cocoa into the boiling water and mix well.

3 Cream the shortening and the sugar. Add the vanilla and beat until light and fluffy. Add the eggs and beat well.

4 Combine together the flour, baking soda, and salt. Add alternately with the buttermilk to the sugar mixture. Blend in the cocoa.

5 Pour the batter into a 9 x 13-inch greased and floured pan.

6 Bake for 35 to 40 minutes or until a tester comes out clean when it is inserted into the center of the cake.

7 Place the cake on a rack and cool for 15 minutes.

Chocolate Decadence Cake

This cake will satisfy even the most hopeless chocoholic.

8 ounces semisweet chocolate chips

1/3 cup espresso coffee (instant espresso is fine)

1 cup butter

1 tablespoon vanilla

6 eggs, separated and at room temperature

1 cup brown sugar

1/2 cup plus 1 tablespoon sugar

1/3 cup all-purpose flour, sifted

1 Preheat the oven to 350° F. Grease and flour a 10-inch spring-form pan.

2 In the top of a double boiler, melt the chocolate chips with the espresso and the butter. Stir until it is smooth. Stir in the vanilla and remove it from the stove.

3 Combine the egg yolks with the brown and white sugar. Beat until the mixture is smooth and ribbons form when the beaters are lifted. Fold the egg yolk mixture into the chocolate and stir in the flour.

4 In another bowl, beat the egg whites until almost stiff. Fold the egg whites into the chocolate mixture and gently combine.

5 Pour the batter into the prepared pan. Bake the cake in the center of the oven for 45 minutes or until a tester comes out clean when inserted in the center of the cake. Cool in the pan on a rack.

Mississippi Mud Cake

Kids love this cake because it's gooey, sticky, and really rich. This recipe and the next are ideal for kids to make themselves.

1/3 cup butter

1 cup sugar

3 eggs

1 cup all-purpose flour

1/2 cup cocoa

1/2 teaspoon baking powder

1/2 teaspoon salt

3/4 cup chopped pecans

1 teaspoon vanilla

3 cups whipped marshmallows (or marshmallow topping)

1 Preheat the oven to 325° F. Grease and lightly flour a 9 x 13-inch baking dish.

2 Cream the butter with the sugar until well blended. Add the eggs one at a time, beating well after each addition.

3 Combine the flour, cocoa, baking powder, and salt. Mix well.

4 Add the flour mixture to the sugar mixture and blend until smooth.

5 Stir in the pecans and the vanilla.

6 Pour the batter into the prepared pan and bake for 15 to 16 minutes or until just set.

7 Remove the cake from the oven and top with the whipped marshmallows. Return it to the oven and bake for about 2 minutes or until the marshmallows are soft.

8 Remove from the oven and drizzle with Chocolate Glaze (see page 113). Cool before serving.

Easy Chocolate Pudding Cake

Serve this warm or right out of the oven.

1 cup all-purpose flour
1 cup sugar
2 tablespoons cocoa
1 1/2 teaspoons baking powder
1/4 teaspoon salt
1/2 cup milk
2 tablespoons canola oil
1 teaspoon vanilla
1 cup brown sugar
1/4 cup cocoa
1 1/2 cups boiling water

1 Preheat the oven to 350° F.

2 Combine the flour, sugar, cocoa, baking powder, and salt.

3 Combine the milk, oil, and vanilla.

4 Add the milk mixture to the sugar mixture and mix well.

5 Pour the batter into a greased 9-inch square baking pan.

6 Combine the brown sugar and the cocoa and sprinkle over the batter.

7 Pour the boiling water over the batter, but do not stir.

8 Bake for 40 minutes or until the cake springs back when lightly touched in the center.

Chocolate Mousse Cake

Of all the chocolate cakes I make, I like this one best. It's a big beautiful cake that is moist and rich. Put a few pieces of shaved bittersweet chocolate on top as a garnish.

8 eggs, separated

3 3/4 cups powdered sugar, divided

1 cup ground almonds

1 cup all-purpose flour

1/3 cup butter, melted and cooled

Mousse

2 cups chopped, unsweetened chocolate

1 cup butter

1 teaspoon instant espresso grains

2 tablespoon coffee liqueur

1 1/4 cup whipping cream

Glaze

1/2 cup whipping cream

2 tablespoons butter

2 cups chopped, unsweetened chocolate

Powdered sugar

1 Preheat the oven to 350° F.

2 Grease two 12 x 17-inch baking sheets and line them with wax paper. Grease the wax paper and lightly dust with flour.

3 Beat the egg yolks with 3 1/2 cups of powdered sugar until pale yellow and ribbons form when the beaters are lifted.

4 Combine the almonds with the flour and fold into the egg mixture.

5 Beat the egg whites until soft peaks form and gently fold into the egg batter. Gently fold the butter into the batter.

6 Pour the batter on the two prepared baking sheets and smooth it out to the edge of the sheets.

7 Bake for about 8 minutes or until a tester comes out clean when inserted into the middle of each cake. Cool on racks. Dust with the remaining powdered sugar. When completely cool, cut out two 8-inch rounds from each sheet cake and set aside. You should have four 8-inch rounds.

The Mousse

1 To make the mousse, combine the chocolate, butter, espresso, and liqueur in a saucepan over low heat. Stir until the chocolate is melted and smooth. Cool to room temperature.

2 Whip the cream until soft peaks form. Gently fold the whipping cream into the chocolate mixture.

3 Place 1 cake layer in the bottom of an 8-inch springform pan. Spoon a third of the mousse over the cake. Top with a second cake layer and a third of the mousse. Top with a third round, then the mousse, ending with the fourth cake on top. Cover with plastic wrap and refrigerate overnight.

4 Release the sides from the springform pan and set the cake on a rack. Pour the glaze (see below) over the top and down the sides of the cake, spreading evenly with a spatula. Refrigerate until the glaze is set. Sift powdered sugar over the cake and serve.

The Glaze

To make the glaze, bring the cream and the butter to a simmer over medium heat. Reduce the heat to low and add the chocolate. Stir until the chocolate has melted and the mixture is smooth and creamy. Cool slightly.

Sour Cream Chocolate Cake

If you like really moist cake, this is the one for you. Sometimes I've been out of sour cream and substituted a 1/2 cup of mayonnaise instead with the same delicious results. If you use mayonnaise, leave out the salt. This can be used as a layer cake or a sheet cake.

1 1/2 cups all-purpose flour

1 cup cocoa

1 1/4 teaspoons baking powder

1 teaspoon baking soda

1/4 teaspoon salt

1 cup sour cream

1/3 cup water

2 teaspoons vanilla

1 cup butter, softened

1 1/3 cups brown sugar

3 eggs

Frosting

1 cup butter, softened

8 ounces cream cheese, at room temperature

4 oz. unsweetened chocolate, melted and cooled

1 teaspoon vanilla

2 1/2 cups powdered sugar

1 Preheat the oven to 350° F.

2 Grease and flour two 9-inch cake pans, or one 9 x 13-inch pan.

3 Sift together the flour, cocoa, baking powder, baking soda, and salt.

4 In another bowl, whisk together the sour cream, water, and vanilla.

5 In a large bowl, cream the butter and brown sugar until light and fluffy.

6 Beat in the eggs, one at a time, mixing well after each addition.

7 Add the flour mixture to the sugar mixture, alternating with the sour cream mixture. Begin and end with the flour mixture. Blend well.

8 Pour the batter into the prepared pans and bake for 25 to 30 minutes or until a tester comes out clean from the center of each cake.

9 Cool in the pans on racks for 15 minutes before turning out onto the racks to cool completely.

Frosting

1 To make the frosting, in a small bowl beat together the butter and cream cheese until light and fluffy.

2 Add the remaining ingredients and beat until creamy.

3 Frost the layer cake and serve.

Cocoa Roll Cake

This is one of my favorite cakes filled with ice cream of any flavor. Put the ice cream into the microwave for a minute or two so it will soften just a bit. Work fast, spreading the ice cream around to cover the sheet cake, leaving a half inch from the edge clear. After rolling up the cake, return it immediately to the freezer to set about an hour. Frost the cake just before serving. At the moment, my favorite filling is chocolate chip mint ice cream, and my favorite frosting is chocolate glaze (see page 113).

1/4 cup boiling water

1/3 cup cocoa

1 1/2 teaspoons vanilla

4 eggs, separated

2/3 cup sugar

1/2 cup cake flour

1/4 teaspoon salt

1/2 teaspoon cream of tartar

1 quart ice cream

1 Preheat the oven to 425° F.

2 Grease a 10 x 17 x 1/2-inch greased baking sheet and line it with wax paper.

3 Coat the paper with cooking spray and dust with flour.

4 Into boiling water, stir the cocoa and vanilla. Mix until smooth and set aside.

5 In a bowl, beat the egg yolks and 1/3 cup of sugar until thick and lemony in color.

6 Add the cocoa mixture and beat until well combined.

7 Add the flour and salt and mix thoroughly.

8 In another bowl, beat the egg whites until foamy. Add the cream of tartar and continue beating until the whites hold soft peaks. Add the remaining 1/3 cup of sugar and beat until stiff, glossy peaks form.

9 Gently fold the egg whites into the cocoa mixture until thoroughly combined.

10 Spoon the batter gently onto the prepared pan and smooth it evenly to all the corners.

11 Bake for 8 minutes or until the cake springs back when touched lightly in the center.

12 Cover the cake with a damp clean towel. When slightly cooled, invert the cake onto the towel and gently peel off the wax paper.

13 Starting with the long side, roll up the cake jelly-roll fashion and cool completely in the towel.

14 After the cake has cooled, it will retain its rolled-up shape even after the towel is removed.

15 See my directions above for working with the ice cream.

Chocolate Chip
Walnut Pound Cake

I like pound cake because once it comes out of the oven, my work is done. Cool and slice it just the way it is.

3 cups all-purpose flour

1/4 teaspoon salt

1/4 teaspoon baking soda

1 cup butter, softened

3 cups sugar

6 eggs

1 cup sour cream

1 tablespoon vanilla

1 1/2 cups semisweet chocolate chips, divided

2 cups chopped walnuts, divided

1 Preheat the oven to 350° F. Grease and flour a 3-quart Bundt pan.

2 Sift together the flour, salt, and baking soda. Set aside.

3 Cream the butter with the sugar until light and fluffy. Add the eggs one at a time, beating well after each addition. Beat in the sour cream and vanilla until well combined.

4 Add the flour mixture and beat at a low speed until just combined. Pour half the batter into the prepared pan and sprinkle about 1/2 of the chips and nuts on top.

5 Pour the remaining batter into the pan and sprinkle the remaining chips and nuts over the top.

6 Bake in the middle of the oven for 1 hour and 20 minutes or until a tester comes out of the center clean.

7 Cool the cake in the pan for about 1 hour and then turn out on a rack to cool completely.

Mocha Fudge Pudding Cake

Coffee and chocolate seem to be made for each other.

1 1/2 cups sugar, divided

1 cup all-purpose flour

2 teaspoons baking powder

1/4 teaspoon salt

1/2 cup butter

2 oz. unsweetened chocolate

1/2 cup milk

1 teaspoon vanilla

1/2 cup brown sugar

1/4 cup cocoa

1/2 cup espresso (instant espresso is fine)

1/2 cup hot water

1 Preheat the oven to 350° F.

2 Combine 1 cup of the sugar, flour, baking powder, and salt. Set aside.

3 Melt the butter and the chocolate in the top of a double boiler over low heat.

4 Combine the flour mixture with the chocolate mixture and mix well. Add the milk and vanilla. Beat until smooth. Pour into a 9-inch greased square baking pan.

5 Combine the remaining 1/2 cup of sugar, the brown sugar, and cocoa in a medium bowl and mix well. Sprinkle evenly over the batter. Heat the espresso but don't boil it. Pour it over the batter, but do not stir.

6 Bake 40 minutes until the center is almost set. Serve warm.

Chocolate Pound Cake

Try dusting a small amount of powdered cocoa through a sieve over the top of the finished cake.

3 cups cake flour

1 cup cocoa

1/2 teaspoon salt

2 cups butter

2 cups sugar

1 tablespoon vanilla

8 eggs

2 tablespoons instant espresso grains

1/4 cup hot water

Powdered sugar

1 Preheat the oven to 350° F. Grease and flour a 3-quart Bundt pan or two loaf pans.

2 Sift the flour with the cocoa and salt. Set aside.

3 In a large bowl, cream the butter and the sugar. Add the vanilla and mix well. Add the eggs one at a time, mixing well after each addition.

4 Combine the flour mixture with the butter mixture.

5 Mix the espresso and the hot water. Blend the espresso into the batter and mix until smooth.

6 Pour the batter into the prepared pan. Bake in the middle of the oven for 1 hour and 20 minutes or until a toothpick comes out clean.

7 Cool the cake in the pan for about 15 minutes and then turn out on a rack to cool completely. Sprinkle with powdered sugar.

Spiced Carrot Cake

I prefer spiced cakes and pies. I love the blend of cinnamon, nut-meg, and cloves. I use lemon cream cheese frosting, page 112.

1 1/2 cups butter

2 cups sugar

4 eggs

2 cups all-purpose flour

2 teaspoons baking soda

1 teaspoon ground cinnamon

1/2 teaspoon ground allspice

1/4 teaspoon ground nutmeg

1/4 teaspoon ground cloves

3 cups grated carrots

1 1/4 cups walnuts, chopped

1/4 cup golden raisins

1 Preheat the oven to 325° F. Grease and flour a 9 x 13-inch bak-ing pan.

2 Cream the butter with the sugar until it is light, fluffy, and a pale yellow color. Add the eggs one at a time. Beat well after each addition.

3 Sift together the flour, baking soda, cinnamon, allspice, nut-meg, and cloves.

4 Add the flour mixture to the butter mixture and blend well. Stir in the carrots, walnuts, and raisins. Spread the batter evenly into the prepared pan. Bake about 45 to 50 minutes or until the cake springs back when gently pressed with the fingers. Cool completely in the pan on a rack.

Easy Does It Spice Cake

Next to chocolate, I would serve spice cake all the time if I thought I could get away with it. I literally baked cake after cake and threw them away until I came up with the right balance for this recipe.

1 cup sugar

1 tablespoon vegetable shortening

2 eggs

1 teaspoon baking soda

1 cup buttermilk

2 cups cake flour

1/2 teaspoon ground cinnamon

1/4 teaspoon ground nutmeg

1/4 teaspoon ground cloves

1/4 teaspoon ground cardamom

1/4 teaspoon salt

1 cup raisins

1 Preheat the oven to 375° F. Grease and flour a 3-quart Bundt pan.

2 Cream the sugar and the shortening until light and fluffy. Add the eggs one at a time, beating well after each addition.

3 Add the baking soda to the buttermilk and stir until it starts to foam. Add the buttermilk to the sugar mixture. Mix well.

4 Sift together the flour with all the spices and salt. Mix in the raisins.

5 Add the flour mixture to the sugar mixture and mix until smooth.

6 Bake for 35 to 40 minutes or until a toothpick comes out clean when inserted in the center. Cool for about 15 minutes in the pan before turning out to cool completely on a rack.

Poppy Seed Cake with
Cream Cheese Frosting

This is a cake that people ask for all the time, particularly for birthdays.
See page 112 for the lemon cream cheese frosting.

1 1/3 cups milk, divided

1/2 cup poppy seeds, divided

2 1/4 cups cake flour

1 tablespoon baking powder

1/4 teaspoon salt

1/2 cup butter, softened

2 teaspoons vanilla

1 1/2 cups sugar, divided

3 egg whites

1 Preheat the oven to 350° F. Grease and flour two 8-inch cake pans. Line the bottom of each pan with wax paper.

2 Bring 2/3 cup milk to a boil over low heat. Stir in 1/3 cup of the poppy seeds. Let cool. Add the remaining milk.

3 Sift together the flour, baking powder, and salt. Set aside.

4 Cream the butter and vanilla with 1 1/4 cups sugar.

5 Add the milk mixture alternately with the flour mixture to the butter and sugar mixture. Do this slowly, adding 1/3 of each mixture at a time. Mix well.

6 Beat the egg whites until they hold soft peaks. Add the remaining sugar a little at a time. Beat until the whites hold stiff glossy peaks. Gently fold the egg whites into the batter.

7 Bake in 2 pans for 30 minutes or until a toothpick inserted in the center comes out clean. Cool in the pans for 15 minutes and then turn out onto racks to cool completely. Frost and dust with the remaining poppy seeds.

Salt-Free, Fat-Free Pineapple
Cake

I developed this cake for a friend who had to go on a special diet and really missed cake. It's so good, you'll forget that it's fat-free.

1 cup pitted prunes

3 tablespoons apple juice

3 1/2 cups shredded carrots

2 cups sugar

1 tablespoon vanilla

4 egg whites, beaten to soft peaks

1 (8-oz.) can crushed pineapple

2 cups all-purpose flour

2 teaspoons baking soda

1 teaspoon ground cinnamon

1/2 teaspoon ground nutmeg

1/2 teaspoon salt

3/4 cup shredded sweetened coconut

1 Preheat the oven to 375° F.

2 Place the pitted prunes and the apple juice in a food processor and process until smooth. Combine the prune purée, carrots, sugar, vanilla, egg whites, and pineapple in a bowl. Stir and let sit for 15 minutes.

3 Sift together the flour, baking soda, cinnamon, nutmeg, and salt.

4 Add the flour mixture to the carrot mixture, stirring until just moistened. Stir in the coconut. Spoon the batter into a greased and floured 10-inch Bundt pan.

5 Bake for 45 minutes. Let cool completely in the pan on a rack. Serve plain or with a lemon cream cheese frosting (see page 112).

Peach Upside-Down Cake

Use clingstone peaches when they are in season. They hold their shape better than the freestone variety.

3/4 cup butter, softened, divided

1/3 cup brown sugar

1 tablespoon dark rum

4 peaches, fresh or canned, peeled and halved

2 1/4 cups all-purpose flour

1 tablespoon baking powder

1 teaspoon salt

2/3 cup sugar

1 egg

1 cup milk

1 Preheat the oven to 375° F. Grease a 9-inch round cake pan.

2 In a small saucepan melt 1/2 cup of the butter with the brown sugar and rum, stirring occasionally. Spread this mixture evenly in the pan and arrange the peach halves.

3 Sift together the flour, baking powder, and salt.

4 Cream the remaining 1/4 cup butter and the sugar in a small bowl until light and fluffy.

5 Beat the egg with the sugar mixture until well combined.

6 Add the flour mixture and the milk alternately with the egg mixture until well blended. Spread the batter evenly over the peaches.

7 Bake for 40 minutes or until a toothpick comes out clean. Immediately invert the cake in one quick motion onto a serving plate. Leave the pan on top of the cake for 30 minutes. Carefully remove the pan and serve.

Pineapple Upside-Down Cake

I think the trick to a good pineapple upside-down cake is fresh pineapple.

2/3 cup butter, divided

1 cup brown sugar

1 pineapple, sliced

10 maraschino cherry halves

3/4 cup sugar, divided

2 eggs, separated

1 teaspoon lemon zest

2 teaspoons fresh lemon juice

1 teaspoon vanilla

1 1/2 cups all-purpose flour

2 teaspoons baking powder

1/4 teaspoon salt

1/2 cup sour cream

1 Preheat the oven to 350° F.

2 In a 10-inch cast-iron skillet melt 1/3 cup of the butter.

3 Remove the skillet from the heat and stir in the brown sugar.

4 Arrange the pineapple slices in the skillet with a cherry half in the center of each slice.

5 Cream the remaining 1/3 cup of butter with 1/2 cup of the granulated sugar.

6 Beat in the egg yolks, lemon zest, lemon juice, and vanilla. Set aside.

7 Combine the flour, baking powder, and salt.

8 Blend the flour mixture into the sugar mixture alternately with the sour cream.

9 Beat the egg whites until soft peaks form. Gradually beat in the remaining 1/4 cup of sugar and beat until stiff peaks form.

10 Fold the egg whites into the batter.

11 Spread the batter evenly over the pineapples in the skillet.

12 Bake about 35 minutes or until the cake springs back when touched lightly in the center.

13 Let stand in the skillet on a rack for at least 15 minutes to cool.

14 Invert onto a serving plate in one quick motion. Serve warm or at room temperature.

Ginger Cake

Nothing makes a statement like the fragrance of gingerbread or ginger cake baking in the oven. A real estate broker told me that when she had to sell a house, she would bake a cake just before a client would come over to look at it. It made the house a home. This is good either with fresh fruit simmered in white wine and honey or French vanilla ice cream.

1/4 cup molasses

1/4 cup sour cream

1/4 cup butter, melted

1/4 cup brown sugar

1 egg

2 teaspoons peeled, grated fresh ginger

1/2 teaspoon lemon zest

1 cup all-purpose flour

1/2 teaspoon baking soda

1/4 teaspoon salt

1 Preheat the oven to 350° F. Grease and flour an 8-inch square baking pan.

2 Combine the molasses, sour cream, butter, sugar, egg, ginger, and lemon zest until smooth. Set aside.

3 Sift together the flour, baking soda, and salt.

4 Combine the flour mixture with the molasses mixture and beat until just combined.

5 Spread the batter evenly in the prepared baking pan.

6 Bake for about 15 to 20 minutes or until a tester comes out clean when inserted in the middle of the cake.

7 Cool the cake in the pan on a rack for 10 minutes. Then turn out onto the rack to cool completely.

Old-Fashioned Applesauce
Cake

This recipe is an old Taylor family favorite. To make a really out-standing cake, make your own raw applesauce. Peel and core about 5 apples. With a steel blade in the food processor, pulse the apples, 1/2 teaspoon of cinnamon, 1/4 teaspoon of cloves, and a pinch of nutmeg to applesauce consistency.

2 1/4 cups all-purpose flour

1 cup sugar

2 teaspoons baking soda

1/4 teaspoon salt

1 teaspoon ground cloves

1 teaspoon ground cinnamon

1/4 teaspoon ground mace

1/4 teaspoon ground nutmeg

1 tablespoon cornstarch

1/4 cup cocoa

1 cup chopped walnuts

1 cup raisins

1 1/2 cups unsweetened applesauce

1/2 cup butter, melted

Powdered sugar

1 Preheat the oven to 325° F. Grease and flour a Bundt pan or a 5 x 9 x 2-inch loaf pan.

2 Sift together the flour, sugar, baking soda, salt, spices, corn-starch, and cocoa. Stir in the remaining ingredients. Mix well.

3 Pour the batter into the prepared pan and bake for 1 hour or until a toothpick comes out clean when inserted in the middle of the cake. Cool the cake in the pan on a rack for 15 minutes and then invert onto a plate to cool completely. Dust with pow-dered sugar.

Almond Spice Pound Cake

Out of the thousand and one variations on pound cake, I like this one best of all.

1 cup sugar

1 cup First Stage Baby Prune Purée

1/4 cup butter

1/2 teaspoon almond extract

1/2 teaspoon vanilla

2 egg whites

1 egg

1 3/4 cups all-purpose flour

2 teaspoons baking powder

1/2 teaspoon ground allspice

1/4 teaspoon salt

1/3 cup milk

1 Preheat the oven to 350°. Grease and flour a 4 x 8 x 3-inch loaf pan.

2 Combine the sugar, prune purée, butter, almond extract, and vanilla. Beat at high speed until light and fluffy. Add the egg whites and egg and continue beating for 3 minutes. Set aside.

3 Mix the flour, baking powder, allspice, and salt. Add the flour mixture to the sugar mixture alternately with the milk, beginning and ending with the flour. Mix well after each addition.

4 Pour into the prepared pan and bake for 1 hour or until a tester comes out clean when inserted in the center. Let cool in the pan 15 minutes before turning out on a rack to cool completely.

Pound Cake

I guarantee you will never taste a better pound cake than this any-where. Sometimes I serve it with fresh strawberries and whipped cream.

1 1/4 cups all-purpose flour

1/4 cup ground pecans

1 teaspoon baking powder

1 cup butter

1 1/4 cups sugar

4 eggs

1/4 teaspoon almond extract

1 Preheat the oven to 350° F.

2 Grease and flour a 4 x 8 x 3-inch loaf pan.

3 Sift the flour and stir in the pecans and baking powder. Set aside.

4 Cream the butter and the sugar until fluffy.

5 Add the eggs one at a time, beating well after each addition.

6 Mix in the almond extract.

7 Fold the flour mixture into the sugar mixture.

8 Pour the batter into the prepared pan.

9 Bake 30 to 40 minutes or until a tester inserted into the middle comes out clean.

10 Cool in the pan for 30 minutes and then turn out onto a rack to cool completely.

Easy Cheesecake with
Champagne Sauce

The champagne sauce with this recipe makes this cheesecake something special. If fresh berries are in season, add a few to the top as a garnish. You can use low-fat sour cream, cream cheese, and cottage cheese without affecting the taste and texture at all.

3 cups graham cracker crumbs

3 tablespoons butter, melted

Filling

1 cup cottage cheese

1 1/2 cups cream cheese, at room temperature

1 1/2 cups sugar

5 eggs

1/4 cup cornstarch

2 cups sour cream

2 tablespoons vanilla

Sauce

1 cup honey

2 cups champagne

1 Preheat the oven to 300° F.

2 Grease the bottom and sides of a 9-inch springform pan.

3 To make the crust, in a food processor combine the graham cracker crumbs and butter. Pulse until the crumbs are well moistened.

4 Press the crumbs onto the bottom and up the sides of the prepared pan to form a thin crust. Bake the crust for 5 minutes and transfer to a rack to cool.

5 To make the filling, purée the cottage cheese in a food processor. Drain for about 30 minutes in cheesecloth set over a small bowl.

6 In a large bowl, blend the cream cheese and the cottage cheese.

7 Add the sugar and mix well.

8 Add the eggs one at a time, blending well after each addition.

9 Sift in the cornstarch and mix.

10 Stir in the sour cream and the vanilla.

11 Pour into the prepared pan and bake for 50 minutes.

12 Turn off the oven and leave the door slightly ajar. Allow the oven and cheesecake to cool completely.

13 Refrigerate 6 hours or overnight before serving.

14 To make the sauce, heat the honey in a heavy saucepan and blend in the champagne.

15 Simmer until thickened to a light syrup, about 30 minutes. Let cool.

16 Spoon some sauce on a plate and place a slice of cheesecake on top.

Almond Torte

This is one great cake. When strawberries first come into season I serve heaps of sliced strawberries and whipped cream over it. The almonds are added as nuts, as paste, and as extract.

1 cup all-purpose flour

1/4 cup ground almonds

1 teaspoon baking powder

3/4 cup butter

1 (7-oz.) package almond paste

3/4 cup sugar

4 eggs

1/2 teaspoon almond extract

1 Preheat the oven to 350° F.

2 Grease a 9-inch cake pan. Line the bottom of the pan with parchment or wax paper. Grease and flour the pan and paper.

3 In a bowl, mix together the flour, almonds, and baking powder. Set aside.

4 In another bowl, cream the butter, almond paste, and sugar until light and fluffy.

5 Add the eggs one at a time, beating well after each addition. Stir in the almond extract.

6 Mix the flour mixture with the sugar mixture until smooth.

7 Pour the batter into the prepared pan and bake for 45 to 50 minutes or until a tester comes out of the center clean.

8 Cool in the pan for several minutes and then remove to a wire rack to cool completely.

Butter Cream Frosting

1/4 cup butter
4 cups powdered sugar
1/4 cup milk
2 teaspoons vanilla

Combine all the ingredients in a bowl. Beat until smooth and creamy. If too stiff, beat in several additional drops of milk. If too creamy, add a little more powdered sugar.

Mocha Frosting

1 cup butter, softened
4 cups powdered sugar
3 tablespoons cocoa
2 tablespoons instant espresso grains
1/4 cup coffee
2 tablespoons Kahlua

Cream the butter with the sugar, cocoa, and espresso. Beat until creamy. Add the coffee and Kahlua. Continue beating until the frosting is creamy and spreadable. Can be used as a filling as well as a frosting.

Chocolate Butter Cream

1/2 cup unsweetened chocolate chips

1 cup butter, softened, divided

1 egg

4 egg yolks

1/2 cup sugar

1/3 cup water

1 teaspoon brandy extract

1 In the top of a double-boiler over hot but not boiling water melt the chocolate and 1/2 cup of the butter. Stir until smooth.

2 Combine the egg and the egg yolks and beat at high speed for 2 minutes.

3 Mix the sugar and the water in a small saucepan and bring to a boil. Boil until the liquid reaches the soft ball stage or about 235° F. on a candy thermometer.

4 While beating the egg mixture at high speed, drizzle the sugar syrup into the egg mixture. Continue beating until the bottom of the bowl is cool to the touch.

5 Gradually beat in the chocolate mixture and the brandy extract until thoroughly blended.

6 While beating the chocolate mixture, add the remaining 1/2 cup butter, one tablespoon at a time.

7 When all the butter has been added, beat for an additional 5 minutes.

8 Refrigerate the butter cream until it is firm enough to spread.

Easy Chocolate Frosting

3 cups sugar

1/2 cup water

2 tablespoons light corn syrup

2 tablespoons butter

4 oz. unsweetened chocolate

2 teaspoons vanilla

1 Over low heat combine all the ingredients except the vanilla in a small saucepan.

2 Cover and bring to a boil.

3 Uncover and cook without stirring until the temperature reaches the soft ball stage, or about 235° F. on a candy ther- mometer.

4 Remove from the heat and cool.

5 Add the vanilla and beat until thick enough to spread.

6 If the frosting is too thick, beat in a little cream. If the frosting is too thin, beat in a little more powdered sugar.

Chocolate Ganache

1/2 cup unsweetened chocolate chips

2 tablespoons butter, softened

1/2 cup whipping cream, whipped

1 In the top of a double boiler over hot but not boiling water, melt the chocolate.

2 Remove from the heat and stir in the butter.

3 Cool thoroughly and then fold in the whipped cream.

4 This can be used as a filling as well as a frosting.

Lemon Cream Cheese Frosting

6 oz. cream cheese, softened

1/4 cup butter, softened

2 cups powdered sugar, sifted

1 tablespoon fresh lemon juice

1 teaspoon lemon zest

1 Cream together the cream cheese and butter.

2 Add the sugar, lemon juice, and zest.

3 Beat until creamy.

Glaceed Cherry Cream Filling

2 cups whipping cream

1/3 cup powdered sugar

1/3 cup (canned) chopped glaceed cherries, drained

1 Whip the cream until soft peaks start to form.

2 Add the sugar and continue whipping until the cream stiffens enough to hold stiff peaks. Do not overbeat.

3 Gently blend in the cherries.

Chocolate Glaze

2 tablespoons butter

2 oz. unsweetened chocolate

1 cup powdered sugar

1 teaspoon vanilla

1/4 cup whipping cream

1 In a double boiler, melt the butter with the chocolate. Stir until smooth and creamy.

2 Remove from the heat and mix in the sugar and vanilla.

3 Stir in the cream and beat until smooth.

Chantilly Cream

Chantilly Cream works better as a frosting than a filling. It doesn't have the body to hold any weight.

1 cup whipping cream
2 tablespoons powdered sugar
1/2 teaspoon vanilla

Whip the cream until it begins to thicken. Add the sugar and the vanilla. Continue beating until stiff peaks are formed, but do not overbeat. Overbeaten whipped cream will become grainy or turn buttery.

Variations

Orange Chantilly Cream

Instead of vanilla, you can use 1 tablespoon of orange liquer and 1 teaspoon orange zest.

Espresso Chantilly Cream

Add 4 tablespoons espresso at room temperature to Chantilly Cream.

Chapter 4

Coffee Cakes & Dessert Breads

The breads in this section are commonly referred to as quick breads. The trick is to mix the dry ingredients until they are well combined. Then quickly add and blend the liquids. Overworking the batter can hurt the finished product, leaving pockets and tunnels of air. Here are some other important tips.

- Even if your bread pan has a nonstick finish, grease and flour the pan.
- Fill the pans one-half to two-thirds full and spread the batter with a spatula to distribute it evenly.
- Always bake the bread in the middle of a preheated oven. The bread is done when a toothpick comes out of the center without crumbs.
- Quick breads are better if they are allowed to age for several hours before serving.
- If wrapped well in plastic wrap or foil, they will stay fresh for several days. I've never really tested this because I usually eat the bread as it comes out of the oven.
- A decorative idea: Bake the quick bread in six-ounce fruit juice cans. Fill the cans three-quarters full so the dough has room to expand while rising. The bread is very attractive when sliced and arranged on a platter.

Cream Cheese Swirl

Coffee Cake

This is perfect for a late afternoon snack. Better yet, finish the cake off with a sugar glaze and serve it for a late supper dessert.

6 oz. cream cheese, softened

2 tablespoons powdered sugar

2 tablespoons fresh lemon juice

2 cups all-purpose flour

1 teaspoon baking soda

1 teaspoon baking powder

1 cup sugar

1/3 cup butter

3 eggs

1 teaspoon vanilla

1/2 cup sour cream

1 tablespoon ground cinnamon

1 cup finely chopped pecans

1/4 cup brown sugar

1 Preheat the oven to 350° F.

2 Grease and flour a 10-inch tube or Bundt pan.

3 Cream the cream cheese with the powdered sugar and lemon juice until smooth. Set aside.

4 Mix together the flour, baking soda, and baking powder. Set aside.

5 Cream the sugar and the butter and mix until smooth.

6 Add the eggs one at a time, mixing well after each addition.

7 Add the vanilla.

8   Add the flour mixture to the sugar mixture alternately with the sour cream. Mix well.

9   Pour half of the batter into the prepared pan.

10 Spoon the cream cheese mixture around the top and pour the rest of the batter over the top to cover.

11 In a small bowl, combine the cinnamon, nuts, and brown sugar.

12 Sprinkle the sugar-nut mixture around the top of the batter lightly pressing the nuts in with the back of a spoon.

13 Bake for 30 to 40 minutes or until a tester inserted into the center comes out clean.

14 Cool in the pan for at least 15 minutes and then turn out onto a rack to cool completely.

Old World Gingerbread

In old England they made this gingerbread in September, stored it in a cool place to ferment, and baked it just before Christmas. If you try it, please let me know how it turns out.

1/2 cup butter
1/2 cup brown sugar
1 cup molasses
3 eggs
3 cups all-purpose flour
2 teaspoons ground ginger
1 teaspoon ground cinnamon
1 teaspoon mace
1 teaspoon ground nutmeg
1 teaspoon baking soda
3/4 cup buttermilk
1/3 cup fresh orange juice
1 teaspoon orange zest
1 cup raisins

1 Preheat the oven to 350° F.

2 Grease and flour a 9 x 13-inch baking pan or dish.

3 In a bowl, cream the butter and the sugar.

4 Stir in the molasses.

5 Beat in the eggs one at a time and set aside.

6 Sift the flour, ginger, cinnamon, mace, nutmeg, and baking soda into a bowl and set aside.

7 Combine the buttermilk, orange juice, orange zest, and raisins in another bowl.

8 Mix the flour mixture into the sugar mixture a third at a time, alternating with the buttermilk mixture.

9 Pour the batter into the prepared pan and bake for 40 to 45 minutes or until a toothpick inserted into the center comes out clean.

10 Cool for 15 minutes on a rack before cutting and serving.

Gingerbread

This is a wonderful, old-fashioned gingerbread.

1/4 cup butter

1/4 cup brown sugar

1/4 cup honey

1/4 cup molasses

2 eggs, beaten

3/4 cup fresh orange juice

2 cups all-purpose flour

1 teaspoon baking powder

1/2 teaspoon salt

1/2 teaspoon baking soda

1 1/2 teaspoons ground ginger

1 teaspoon ground cinnamon

1 teaspoon ground nutmeg

1 teaspoon orange zest

1 cup raisins

1 Preheat the oven to 350° F. Grease an 8 x 8-inch square pan.

2 In a bowl, cream the butter and brown sugar until smooth and thick. Add the honey and molasses. Beat until smooth. Add the eggs with the orange juice. Stir well.

3 In another bowl, combine the flour, baking powder, salt, baking soda, ginger, cinnamon, and nutmeg. Stir in the orange zest.

4 Add the flour mixture to the butter mixture. Add the raisins and stir until well blended.

5 Pour the batter into the greased pan and bake for 40 minutes or until a toothpick inserted into the center comes out clean. Cool in the pan on a rack at least 15 minutes before cutting and serving. Serve warm.

Lemon Bread with Lemon Glaze

This is great bread to start the day with coffee, or with tea in the afternoon. For increased lemon flavor, add some lemon zest to the batter along with the pecans.

2 cups all-purpose flour

1 teaspoon baking powder

1/2 teaspoon baking soda

1/4 teaspoon salt

1 1/2 cups sugar

1/2 cup butter, softened

3 eggs

1/3 cup fresh lemon juice

1/2 cup milk

1 cup chopped pecans

1 cup powdered sugar

1 tablespoon fresh lemon juice

1 Preheat the oven to 350° F. Grease and flour a 5 x 9-inch loaf pan.

2 Sift together the flour, baking powder, baking soda, and salt. Set aside.

3 Cream the sugar and the butter until smooth and fluffy. Add the eggs one at a time, blending well after each addition. Gradually blend in the lemon juice.

4 Add the milk alternately with the flour mixture and stir well. Add the pecans. Pour the batter into the prepared pan and bake for 50 to 55 minutes until a tester comes out clean when inserted into the center of the loaf. Remove from the oven and cool for 15 minutes in the pan, then remove to a rack to cool completely.

5 Combine the sugar and the lemon juice in a small saucepan and over low heat dissolve the sugar. Heat for just a minute or two longer and remove from the heat. Let cool slightly before drizzling over the bread in a decorative pattern.

Pumpkin Nut Bread

This recipe can be made with fresh pumpkin as well as canned. Cut the pumpkin into quarters. Bake it in the oven at 350° F. until soft, about 45 to 60 minutes. Scrape out and mash the flesh. This recipe makes two loaves.

3 1/2 cups all-purpose flour

2 teaspoons baking soda

1 1/2 teaspoons ground cinnamon

1/2 teaspoon baking powder

2 cups sugar

2/3 cup butter

4 eggs

2 cups canned or fresh baked pumpkin

1/2 cup water

1 cup chopped pecans

1 teaspoon orange zest

1 Preheat the oven to 350° F. Grease and flour two 5 x 9-inch loaf pans.

2 Combine the flour, baking soda, cinnamon, and baking powder. Set aside.

3 Cream the sugar and butter until smooth and fluffy. Add the eggs one at a time, mixing well after each addition. Add the pumpkin and the water. Mix until smooth.

4 Stir in the flour mixture with the pumpkin mixture. Add the nuts and the orange zest.

5 Pour half of the mixture into each of the prepared pans and bake for 55 to 60 minutes or until a tester inserted into the center of each loaf comes out clean. Cool 15 minutes in the pans before removing to racks to cool completely.

Chocolate Chip Banana Bread

This is one of my favorites. It must be the chocolate chips. The combination of chocolate and banana has always been a winner.

2 cups all-purpose flour

1 teaspoon baking powder

1/2 teaspoon salt

1/2 teaspoon baking soda

1 cup sugar

1 1/4 cups mashed ripe bananas

1/2 cup butter

2 eggs

1 1/2 cups mini semisweet chocolate chips

1/2 cup chopped walnuts

1 Preheat the oven to 350° F.

2 Grease the bottom only of a 5 x 9-inch loaf pan.

3 Combine the flour, baking powder, salt, and baking soda in a bowl. Set aside.

4 Cream the sugar with the bananas and butter.

5 Add the eggs one at a time, mixing well after each addition.

6 Combine the flour mixture with the banana mixture. Add the chips and the nuts.

7 Pour the batter into the prepared pan and bake for 60 to 70 minutes or until a tester comes out of the center of the loaf clean. Cool for 15 minutes in the pan, then turn out onto a rack to cool completely.

Chocolate Marble Loaf

This is a quick and easy bread that can be served anytime.

1 tablespoon instant espresso grains

3 tablespoons coffee

3 tablespoons cocoa

1 tablespoon molasses

2 1/2 cups all-purpose flour

1 cup sugar

1/4 cup brown sugar

1 1/2 teaspoons baking powder

1 teaspoon baking soda

1/4 teaspoon salt

1 cup applesauce

1/3 cup plain yogurt

1/3 cup canola oil

1/4 teaspoon vanilla

2 eggs

Powdered sugar (optional)

1 Preheat the oven to 350° F.

2 Grease a 5 x 9-inch loaf pan and set aside.

3 Mix the espresso into the coffee.

4 Combine the coffee, cocoa, and molasses. Stir and set aside.

5 Combine the flour, sugars, baking powder, baking soda, and salt in a large bowl. Make a well in the center of the mixture.

6 In another bowl, mix together the applesauce, yogurt, oil, vanilla, and eggs until well blended.

7 Add this to the flour mixture by pouring it into the center of the well and mixing from the inside out until all the dry ingredients are incorporated and the batter is smooth.

8 Remove 1 cup of the batter and combine it with the cocoa mixture, mixing until smooth.

9 Spoon the cocoa batter alternately with the applesauce batter into the prepared pan.

10 Using the tip of a knife, swirl the batters together.

11 Bake for 1 hour or until a tester comes out clean when inserted into the center of the loaf.

12 Let set in the pan for 10 minutes before turning out onto a rack to cool completely.

13 Sift the powdered sugar over the top of the loaf.

Southern Banana Bread

The addition of the Southern Comfort makes this banana bread really different. This recipe makes two loaves.

3 cups mashed bananas

2 tablespoons Southern Comfort

1 cup sugar

3 eggs

3/4 cup butter, melted and cooled

2 cups all-purpose flour

2 teaspoons baking soda

1/4 cup buttermilk

1 cup chopped pecans

1 Preheat the oven to 350° F.

2 Grease and flour two 5 x 9-inch loaf pans and set aside.

3 Combine the bananas, Southern Comfort, sugar, and eggs. Gradually add the butter, stirring continually until the mixture is smooth and well blended.

4 Mix together the flour and the baking soda.

5 Mix the flour mixture with the banana mixture.

6 Stir in the buttermilk and then fold in the pecans.

7 Pour the batter into the prepared pans and bake for about 45 minutes.

8 Remove the loaves from the pans and set on racks until cooled completely.

Chapter 5

Desserts You Eat with a Spoon

This is the section where we put all the desserts I love but couldn't find a category for. I've included the best of my mousses, bread puddings, and a wonderful crème brûlée.

When making the puddings you may want to scald the milk first as it will cut down on the cooking time. If you use milk right out of the carton, add about 10 minutes to the cooking time. What I like about puddings is you just throw all the ingredients together and bake the dish. Remember to keep puddings chilled to 40° F., as they can become contaminated by bacteria.

In California we have a large variety of fresh fruits available to us year around. Here are a few hints that may help you.

• I try to stay in sync with the seasons and therefore avoid buying fruit that has been kept in cold storage for a long period of time.

• I like to choose fruit that is ripe and ready to eat that day.

• I look for fruit that is the right color. For instance, bright red apples, deep orange-colored oranges and tangerines, and bright yellow lemons.

• I feel and smell melons at the point where the vine was cut to determine their freshness. If you can smell the melon, it is probably sweet and juicy.

• I look for pineapples that are golden and have a little give to them when squeezed. You can smell these as well. A ripe pineapple is intensely fragrant. Also feel the pineapple. It shouldn't be too soft.

• I don't buy pears in the spring or early summer because they are a fall and early winter fruit.

• I don't buy watermelon in the winter because the best water-melons will be ready in the middle to late summer.

• Berries are at their best from about the end of June to the late fall.

Bread Pudding with
Apples, Raisins, & Dates

I've tried a lot of bread puddings over the years. This is my favorite. It's a good way to use up those odds and ends of bread that seem to get left over.

2/3 cup raisins

1/3 cup chopped dates

1/4 cup brandy

15 slices white bread, crusts removed

1/2 cup butter, softened

1/2 cup sugar

3 eggs

1 egg yolk

1/2 cup whipping cream

1 1/2 cups milk, scalded

2 teaspoons lemon zest

1 teaspoon vanilla

1 cup peeled, chopped apple

1 Combine the raisins, dates, and brandy in a small bowl. Let stand for 30 minutes.

2 Preheat the oven to 350° F.

3 Butter the bottom and sides of a 9 x 13-inch baking dish.

4 Butter one side of the bread slices generously with the butter, and cut into 1-inch squares. Spread evenly in the prepared pan.

5 Mix the sugar, eggs, and egg yolk in a bowl.

6 Whisk in the cream, milk, zest, and vanilla.

7 Stir in the apples and brandy mixture.

8 Pour over the bread and shake the dish gently to let the ingre-dients settle. Let stand for 15 minutes.

9 Set the pan in a larger baking pan and add enough hot water to come 2/3 up the sides of the smaller dish.

10 Bake until the pudding is set and lightly browned, about 35 to 45 minutes.

11 Remove from the oven and serve warm.

Bread and Butter Pudding

This pudding is more traditional than the preceding one.

15 slices soft white bread, crusts removed

1/2 cup butter, soft

1/2 cup golden raisins

1/2 cup dried currants

1 cup milk

2 cups whipping cream

1 teaspoon vanilla

4 eggs

1/4 cup plus 1 tablespoon sugar

1/4 teaspoon nutmeg

1 tablespoon fresh lemon juice

1 Preheat the oven to 325° F.

2 Butter the bottom and sides of a 9 x 13-inch baking dish.

3 Generously spread both sides of the bread with the remaining butter.

4 Layer the bread in the prepared pan, sprinkling each layer evenly with the raisins and the currants.

5 Scald the milk and cream in a saucepan over medium heat.

6 Remove from the heat and whisk in the vanilla.

7 Let the mixture stand for about 15 minutes.

8 Bring the mixture back to simmer.

9 Whisk together the eggs, sugar, and nutmeg until smooth.

10 Gradually whisk in the hot milk in a thin stream.

11 Return the mixture to the saucepan and stir over low heat, about 10 minutes, until the custard thickens and lightly coats the back of a metal spoon. Do not boil.

12 Pour the custard over the bread, making sure the bread is immersed completely. Let it soak for 30 minutes.

13 Set the baking dish in a larger pan and add enough hot water to the large pan to come 2/3 up the sides of the smaller pan.

14 Bake until the pudding is set, about 45 minutes.

15 Remove from the oven. Lightly sprinkle the lemon juice evenly over the top and serve.

Maple Bread Pudding

This bread pudding is exceptional. I'd serve it warm from the oven.

15 slices white bread, crusts removed

2 cups milk, scalded

1 cup whipping cream

1/3 cup maple syrup

2 tablespoons sugar

1 teaspoon vanilla

1 teaspoon ground cinnamon

1/4 teaspoon ground nutmeg

3 eggs

1/2 cup golden raisins

1 Preheat the oven to 325° F.

2 Dice the bread into 1-inch squares and spread in a single layer on a cookie sheet. Toast for 10 minutes. Watch closely so as not to burn the bread.

3 Remove from the oven and place the bread in a well-greased 9 x 13-inch baking dish.

4 Increase the oven heat to 350° F.

5 Combine the milk, cream, maple syrup, sugar, vanilla, cinnamon, nutmeg, and eggs.

6 With a wire whisk, mix until well blended and stir in the raisins.

7 Pour the mixture over the bread, tossing gently to coat. Let the mixture stand for 30 minutes.

8 Bake for 1 hour or until the pudding is set.

9 Serve warm.

Lemon Custard

This is a good "make ahead" dessert. It's light and is perfect with fresh raspberries or blueberries.

10 egg yolks
3/4 cup sugar
1/4 cup fresh lemon juice
1 teaspoon brandy extract
2 teaspoons lemon zest
1 cup whipped cream, chilled

1 Whisk the egg yolks and sugar together in the top of a double boiler over very hot but not boiling water.

2 Heat until the mixture begins to thicken, about 5 minutes.

3 Add the lemon juice, brandy extract, and zest. Continue cooking for 5 more minutes.

4 Pour the mixture into a large bowl and let cool completely, stirring occasionally.

5 Fold the chilled whipped cream into the lemon mixture.

6 Cover and chill for about 3 hours.

Rice Pudding with Dried Cherries

The cherries make this rice pudding special.

1 cup cooked short-grain rice

1 cup dried bing cherries

2 cups milk, scalded

2 cups whipping cream

1/3 cup sugar

1 teaspoon vanilla

1/3 cup maple syrup

1 teaspoon brandy extract

2 eggs

1 Preheat the oven to 350° F. Grease a 9 x 13-inch baking dish.

2 Cover the bottom evenly with the rice and cherries.

3 In a heavy bottomed saucepan, combine the milk, cream, sugar, and vanilla. Over low heat bring to a boil. Stir in the maple syrup and the extract.

4 Whip the eggs, adding 1/4 cup of the milk mixture while continuing to beat.

5 Add the rest of the hot milk mixture in a thin stream. Mix until smooth.

6 Pour the custard over the cherries and rice and let sit for 30 minutes.

7 Bake for 1 hour or until the pudding is set in the middle.

Chocolate Mousse

This is the simplest mousse recipe I've seen short of getting it out of a box. The flavor is rich and smooth.

6 oz. unsweetened chocolate

4 egg whites

1 cup whipping cream

1 teaspoon vanilla

1 cup powdered sugar

1 In the top of a double boiler, melt the chocolate over hot but not boiling water. Stir until smooth and let cool slightly.

2 Beat the egg whites until stiff peaks form and set aside.

3 In a separate bowl, whip the cream until soft peaks begin to form. Add the vanilla and the sugar and continue beating until the cream just begins to stiffen. Do not overbeat.

4 Gently fold the egg whites into the whipped cream.

5 Add the cooled chocolate and quickly fold it in until well blended and smooth.

6 Spoon the mousse into individual serving bowls and refrigerate at least 2 hours before serving.

Dark Chocolate Crème Brûlée

Crème brûlée is easy to make but it needs attention. You have to stir it constantly, but it's worth it. Here's a particularly good recipe.

3 cups whipping cream

10 oz. semisweet chocolate

1 tablespoon instant espresso grains

10 egg yolks

3 tablespoons Kahlua

Sugar

1 Combine the cream, chocolate, and espresso in the top of a double boiler over hot but not boiling water.

2 Stir until the chocolate is melted and the mixture is smooth.

3 Beat the egg yolks and the Kahlua together in a large bowl.

4 Whisk in half of the chocolate mixture.

5 Add the chocolate/Kahlua mixture to the chocolate in the double boiler and stir until thickened, about 10 to 15 minutes.

6 Strain out all the lumps and divide the mixture among individual ramekins or small serving bowls.

7 Cover and refrigerate at least 3 hours.

8 Preheat the broiler.

9 Sprinkle the top of each custard evenly with 1 teaspoon sugar.

10 Broil the custard 2 inches from the heat source until the sugar is caramelized, about 30 seconds to 1 minute. Watch carefully so as not to burn the sugar and custard. Instead of putting the crème brûlée under the broiler, I sometimes use a hand-held gas torch. You have more control over the heat source. However, because the flame is not quite as hot, it takes longer to caramelize the sugar. It's a handy tool to add to your kitchen supplies, but does take a little practice.

11 To keep the custard cold while it is in the broiler, pack ice around the base of the serving bowls so that the melted ice can drain away from the custard.

Key Lime Mousse

This is a refreshing change of pace. Use fresh lime juice with a little fresh lime zest for a summertime dessert.

1 cup fresh lime juice, divided

1 envelope unflavored gelatin

1 teaspoon lime zest

4 eggs, separated and at room temperature

1 cup sugar, divided

1 cup whipped cream, chilled

Toasted coconut

1 Combine 2 tablespoons of the lime juice with the gelatin in a small bowl for 5 minutes.

2 In a medium saucepan, combine the rest of the lime juice and the zest with the egg yolks and beat until creamy and a light lemon color. Add 3/4 cup of the sugar. Cook over low heat until the mixture thickens slightly, stirring constantly, for about 10 minutes. Remove from the heat.

3 Add the gelatin and stir to dissolve. Pour into a large bowl and cool to lukewarm.

4 In another bowl, beat the egg whites until soft peaks start to form. Add the remaining sugar and continue beating until the peaks stiffen.

5 Fold the whites into the whipped cream.

6 Gently fold the cream mixture into the lime mixture.

7 Divide between individual serving bowls, cover, and refrigerate about 4 hours or until firm. Top each mousse with a dollop of whipped cream, sprinkled with shredded, toasted coconut.

Frozen Chocolate Mousse

I love chocolate mousse. Add fresh strawberries and you have a perfect combination.

3 cups quartered strawberries

1/4 cup powdered sugar

1/2 teaspoon vanilla

3/4 cup chopped milk chocolate

2 tablespoons water

1 teaspoon instant espresso grains

3 eggs, separated and at room temperature

1 cup whipped cream, chilled

1 Combine the strawberries, sugar, and vanilla. Toss well to coat. Cover and chill.

2 Melt the chocolate with the water and espresso in the top of a double boiler over hot but not boiling water. Stir until smooth.

3 Whisk in the egg yolks one at a time.

4 Remove the pan from the heat and cool to lukewarm.

5 Beat the egg whites until stiff peaks form.

6 Fold a quarter of the whites into the chocolate mixture.

7 Gently fold in the remaining whites.

8 Spoon the mousse into 4 dessert cups and freeze for at least 2 hours.

9 Top each cup of mousse with the strawberries and a dollop of whipped cream.

Ginger & Lime Honeydew
Melon Compote

This is a refreshing way to end a rich dinner. This dish should be made ahead of time to give the mint and spice a chance to settle in and the fruit a chance to chill. Keep it covered in the refrigerator until ready to serve. Toss it one final time before serving.

2 teaspoons lime zest

1/3 cup fresh lime juice

1/4 cup sugar

1 tablespoon fresh grated ginger

1/3 cup water

1 honeydew melon, flesh scooped into balls

2 tablespoons minced mint leaves

1 In a saucepan, combine the zest, lime juice, sugar, ginger, and water.

2 Bring to a boil, stirring until the sugar is dissolved.

3 Boil for another 5 minutes or until the sauce thickens slightly.

4 Remove from the heat and set aside to cool.

5 In a serving bowl, toss the melon balls with the sauce and the mint.

6 Cover and chill for at least 2 hours before serving.

Cantaloupe with Port Gelatin

Not only is this dessert good, it's attractive as well. The port gives this sauce a rich full-bodied taste.

1 envelope unflavored gelatin

1/4 cup cold water

2 cantaloupes

1 cup Ruby Port

1/3 cup fresh lemon juice

1/2 cup sugar

1 In a bowl, sprinkle the gelatin over the water and let it soften for 10 minutes.

2 Cut the cantaloupes in half and discard the seeds.

3 In a small saucepan, combine the Port, lemon juice, and sugar. Heat the mixture over medium high heat until the sugar dissolves. Continue cooking for another 3 to 5 minutes, stirring constantly. Add the gelatin and reduce the heat to low. Cook until the gelatin dissolves.

4 Set the saucepan in a pan filled with ice and continue stirring until the mixture has reached room temperature but not set.

5 Divide it between the cantaloupe halves. Cover the cantaloupe with plastic wrap and chill for 3 hours to overnight. Carefully remove the plastic wrap. Cut each cantaloupe lengthwise into 2 pieces and lightly sprinkle with salt. Serve chilled.

Poached Pears

When pears first come into season it's the time to make this dessert. I like to buy them just a little unripe. They will soften as they simmer.

4 firm Bartlett pears

2 cups cranberry juice

1 cup sugar

2 bay leaves

3 whole cloves

2 teaspoons orange zest

Bay leaves

1 Peel the pears and cut them in half, leaving the stems intact.

2 Core the pears with a melon-ball scoop.

3 To a large saucepan, add the cranberry juice, sugar, bay leaves, cloves, and orange zest.

4 Add the pears and simmer uncovered, turning occasionally.

5 Cook for 10 to 15 minutes or until the pears are tender but still firm.

6 Reserve the poaching liquid.

7 Transfer the pears to a serving plate and chill, covered, for 2 hours.

8 Boil the reserved liquid until reduced to about 1 cup.

9 Strain the liquid through a fine sieve and chill the reduced liquid in a bowl of ice water. Stir the liquid until cooled.

10 Pour over the pears, garnish with additional bay leaves, and serve.

Poached Pears with
Caramel Sauce

This is my favorite fruit dessert recipe. I look for firm, slightly under-ripe pears so they don't get mushy during cooking.

4 Bartlett pears, ripe but firm

1/4 cup fresh lemon juice

6 cups water

2 cups sugar

2 teaspoons vanilla

1 cup whipping cream

1 Peel the pears and halve them lengthwise.

2 Core the pears with a melon-ball scoop.

3 Wash the pears in a bowl of water mixed with the lemon juice.

4 In a skillet large enough to hold the pears in a single layer, combine the water with the sugar and vanilla.

5 Bring the mixture to a boil, stirring until the sugar is dissolved.

6 Add the pears and simmer for 8 to 10 minutes, or until they are just tender.

7 Transfer the pears to a serving platter and set aside.

8 Continue cooking the liquid over moderate-high heat, stirring constantly, until the liquid is a golden caramel color.

9 Remove from the heat and carefully stir in the cream.

10 Return to the heat and lightly boil the sauce until it is reduced by about half.

11 Spoon the caramel sauce over the pears and serve.

Honeydew Compote with
Lime, Basil, and Mint

The basil in this compote gives this dessert a refreshing taste. Make it far enough ahead so it has time to chill before serving.

1 honeydew melon, flesh scooped into balls

2 tablespoons fresh lime juice

1 tablespoon minced fresh basil

1 tablespoon minced fresh mint

Sugar, to taste

In a bowl combine all the ingredients. Mix, cover, and chill.

Orange and Kiwi Compote
with Strawberry Sauce

You can use apples and oranges, or mixed melons in this compote.

2 cups fresh strawberries

2 tablespoons orange liqueur

1/4 cup sugar

1 teaspoon orange zest

6 oranges, sectioned and seeded

4 kiwi, peeled and diced

Fresh mint leaves

Place the strawberries, liqueur, sugar, and zest in a processor or blender. Process until smooth. Chill for at least 30 minutes. Mix the oranges and kiwi together. Divide the fruit between four small bowls. Top with chilled sauce, garnish with a mint leaf, and serve.

Peaches and Raspberries in
Spiced White Wine

You can substitute champagne for the white wine in this recipe for a more festive occasion.

3 cups dry white wine, divided

1/2 cup sugar

2 teaspoons orange zest

3 cinnamon sticks

6 peaches, blanched, peeled, and sliced thin

4 cups fresh raspberries

1 Combine 1 cup of the wine, sugar, zest, and cinnamon in a saucepan.

2 Over low heat stir until the sugar has melted.

3 Increase the heat to medium and simmer for 15 minutes.

4 Remove from the heat and stir in the remaining wine.

5 Mix the peaches with the raspberries and add them to the wine mixture. Toss to coat.

6 Cover and refrigerate for at least 1 hour.

7 Divide the fruit and wine among four glass goblets and serve.

Marinated Strawberries
in Orange Liqueur

Orange liqueur seems to make every compote special. It is perfect in this recipe with the strawberries.

4 cups fresh strawberries, quartered

1 cup powdered sugar

1/4 cup Grand Marnier or Triple Sec, divided

1 cup vanilla flavored frozen yogurt, softened

1 cup whipped cream

1 teaspoon fresh lemon juice

1 Combine the strawberries, sugar, and 2 tablespoons of the liqueur.

2 Toss gently, cover, and chill for 30 minutes.

3 Stir the yogurt until smooth and fold into the whipped cream.

4 Add the remaining liqueur and lemon juice to the yogurt mixture and stir well.

5 Divide the fruit between six small bowls or stem glasses. Top with the yogurt mixture and serve.

Strawberries and Raspberries
in a Custard Sauce

This is an all-time great summer dessert. Use berries that are really ripe, big, and firm.

1 1/2 cups milk

1/3 cup sugar

1 tablespoon flour

4 egg yolks

1 teaspoon vanilla

2 cups fresh strawberries, halved

2 cups fresh raspberries

1/4 cup powdered sugar

Fresh mint leaves

1 Combine the milk, sugar, flour, and egg yolks in the top of a double boiler.

2 Cook over hot but not boiling water for about 40 minutes, stirring continually. The mixture should end up thick enough to coat a metal spoon.

3 Mix in the vanilla.

4 Pour the custard into six individual serving bowls or stem glasses.

5 Let the custard cool to room temperature, cover, and chill.

6 Mix the fruit and toss with the sugar. Chill for 30 minutes.

7 Top the custard with the fruit and garnish with a mint leaf.

Dried Fruit Compote

I like this dessert because it's not limited by the season, and it simply tastes good.

1/3 pound chopped dried prunes

1 cup dried peaches

1 cup dried apples

1 cup dried apricots

1 fresh lemon, sliced thin

1 teaspoon vanilla

3 cups apple juice

1 cup water

3/4 cup brown sugar

1 Combine all the dried fruit and lemon in a large bowl.

2 Add the vanilla and toss to coat. Set aside.

3 Combine the apple juice, water, and sugar in a saucepan. Bring to a boil and cook for 1 minute.

4 Pour the sauce over the dried fruit, cover, and chill for 8 hours.

5 Preheat the oven to 375° F.

6 Add the fruit to a small casserole dish and bake it, covered, for 30 minutes.

7 Stir every 10 minutes or so.

8 Serve either warm or chilled.

Raspberries with **Ruby Port**
and Cream

I like this recipe because I don't have to wait until summer to enjoy it. The first time I tried it I couldn't believe what I was eating, it tasted so good.

3 cups frozen raspberries, thawed and divided

1/4 cup Ruby Port

1/2 cup powdered sugar, divided

1 teaspoon vanilla

2 cups whipped cream

1 Add 1 cup of the berries to the food processor fitted with a steel blade.

2 Pulse until the berries are liquefied.

3 Mix the whole berries with the processed berries.

4 Add the Port and 1/4 cup sugar.

5 Add the sugar and vanilla to the whipped cream and gently stir.

6 Add the berry mixture to the cream mixture.

7 Pour the berries into six individual serving bowls or stem glasses and chill for 3 hours before serving.

Index

A

Absolute Best Cappuccino Brownies, 29
Almond Spice Pound Cake, 104
Almond Torte, 108
Amaretto Pumpkin Pie, 75

B

bars, 6
  Chocolate Chip Pecan Squares, 36
  Easy Butterscotch Bars, 42
  Ginger Shortbread, 41
  Hazelnut Shortbread, 41
  Lemon Bars, 43
  Macadamia Coconut Bars, 44
  Oatmeal Chocolate Squares, 38
  Orange Shortbread, 41
  Out of This World Spice Bars, 37
  Spicy Shortbread, 41
  Super Easy Shortbread, 39
Basic Sugar Cookies, 22
Berry Pie, 73
Blackberry/Peach Crisp, 77
Boysenberry Cobbler, 76
Brandied Fruit Pie, 62
Bread and Butter Pudding, 130
Bread Pudding with Apples, Raisins, & Dates, 128
brownies, 7
  Absolute Best Cappuccino Brownies, 29
  Espresso Brownies with a Coffee Liqueur Glaze, 33
  Mint Chocolate Brownies, 35
  Super Rich Chocolate Brownies, 32
Butter Cream Frosting, 109
Butterscotch Cookies, 23

C

Cantaloupe with Port Gelatin, 141
cakes, 81

Almond Spice Pound Cake, 104
Almond Torte, 108
  Chocolate Chip Walnut Pound Cake, 92
  Chocolate Decadence Cake, 83
  Chocolate Mousse Cake, 86
  Chocolate Pound Cake, 94
  Cocoa Roll Cake, 90
  Easy Cheesecake with Champagne Sauce, 106
  Easy Chocolate Pudding Cake, 85
  Easy Does It Spice Cake, 96
  Easy & Fast Chocolate Cake, 82
  Ginger Cake, 102
  Mississippi Mud Cake, 84
  Mocha Fudge Pudding Cake, 93
  Old-Fashioned Applesauce Cake, 103
  Peach Upside-Down Cake, 99
  Pineapple Upside-Down Cake, 100
  Poppy Seed Cake with Cream Cheese Frosting, 97
  Pound Cake, 105
  Salt-Free, Fat-Free Pineapple Cake, 98
  Sour Cream Chocolate Cake, 88
  Spiced Carrot Cake, 95
Chantilly Cream, 114
Chocolate Butter Cream, 110
Chocolate Chip Banana Bread, 123
Chocolate Chip Cookies, 16
Chocolate Chip and Peanut Cookies, 19
Chocolate Chip Pecan Squares, 36
Chocolate Chip Walnut Pound Cake, 92
Chocolate Chunk Pecan Pie, 67
Chocolate Cookies with a White Filling, 26
Chocolate Crispy Cookies, 23
Chocolate Decadence Cake, 83

Chocolate Filling, 9
Chocolate Ganache, 112
Chocolate Glaze, 113
Chocolate Marble Loaf, 124
Chocolate Mousse, 135
Chocolate Mousse Cake, 86
Chocolate Mousse Pie, 72
Chocolate Pound Cake, 94
Classic American Apple Pie, 50
cobblers, 45
    Blackberry/Peach Crisp, 77
    Boysenberry Cobbler, 76
    Fast Cherry Cobbler, 78
    Fast Peach Cobbler, 80
    Peach/Apple Crisp, 79
Cocoa Roll Cake, 90
coffee cakes, 115
    Cream Cheese Swirl Coffee Cake,
        116
cookies, 5-6
    Basic Sugar Cookies, 22
    Butterscotch Cookies, 23
    Chocolate Chip Cookies, 16
    Chocolate Chip and Peanut
        Cookies, 19
    Chocolate Cookies with a White
        Filling, 26
    Chocolate Crispy Cookies, 23
    Easy & Fast Buttery Cookies, 8
    Easy and Fast Ginger Snaps, 28
    Easy Double Chocolate Cookies,
        18
    Fast Wheat Germ Cookies, 10
    Great Grandma's Ginger Cookies,
        25
    Molasses Cookies, 24
    New England Maple Cookies, 13
    Peanut Butter Cookies, 14
    Peanutty Chocolate Cookies, 15
    Pecan & White Chocolate Chip
        Oatmeal Cookies, 20
    Poppy Seed Cookies, 11
    Southern Brown Sugar Cookies, 12
    Spice Cookies, 23

White Chocolate Chip Cookies with
    Macadamia Nuts, 21
Cream Cheese Swirl Coffee Cake,
    116
Crustless Coconut Pecan Pie, 70

D
Dark Chocolate Crème Brûlée, 136
dessert breads, 115
    Chocolate Chip Banana Bread, 123
    Chocolate Marble Loaf, 124
    Gingerbread, 120
    Lemon Bread with Lemon Glaze,
        121
    Old World Gingerbread, 118
    Pumpkin Nut Bread, 122
    Southern Banana Bread, 126
desserts you eat with a spoon, 127
    Bread and Butter Pudding, 130
    Bread Pudding with Apples,
        Raisins, & Dates, 128
    Cantaloupe with Port Gelatin, 141
    Chocolate Mousse, 135
    Dark Chocolate Crème Brûlée, 136
    Dried Fruit Compote, 148
    Frozen Chocolate Mousse, 139
    Ginger & Lime Honeydew Melon
        Compote, 140
    Honeydew Compote with Lime,
        Basil, and Mint, 144
    Key Lime Mousse, 138
    Lemon Custard, 133
    Maple Bread Pudding, 132
    Marinated Strawberries in Orange
        Liqueur, 146
    Orange and Kiwi Compote with
        Strawberry Sauce, 144
    Peaches and Raspberries in Spiced
        White Wine, 145
    Poached Pears, 142
    Poached Pears with Caramel
        Sauce, 143
    Raspberries with Ruby Port and
        Cream, 149

Strawberries and Raspberries in a Custard Sauce, 147
Deep Dish Peach Pie, 59
Dried Fruit Compote, 148
Dutch Apple Raisin Pie, 52

E

Easy Butterscotch Bars, 42
Easy Cheesecake with Champagne Sauce, 106
Easy Chocolate Frosting, 111
Easy Chocolate Pudding Cake, 85
Easy Does It Spice Cake, 96
Easy Double Chocolate Cookies, 18
Easy & Fast Buttery Cookies, 8
Easy & Fast Chocolate Cake, 82
Easy and Fast Ginger Snaps, 28
Espresso Brownies with a Coffee Liqueur Glaze, 33
Espresso Chantilly Cream, 114

F

Fast Cherry Cobbler, 78
Fast Peach Cobbler, 80
Fast Wheat Germ Cookies, 10
Flaky Pie Crust, 46
fillings, 81
    Chantilly Cream, 114
    Chocolate Filling, 9
    Espresso Chantilly Cream, 114
    Glaceed Cherry Cream Filling, 113
    Orange Chantilly Cream, 114
frostings, 81
    Butter Cream Frosting, 109
    Chocolate Butter Cream, 110
    Chocolate Ganache, 112
    Easy Chocolate Frosting, 111
    Lemon Cream Cheese Frosting, 112
    Mocha Frosting, 109
    Vanilla Frosting, 9
Frozen Chocolate Mousse, 139

G

Gingerbread, 120

Ginger Cake, 102
Ginger & Lime Honeydew Melon Compote, 140
Ginger Peach Pie, 60
Ginger Shortbread, 41
Glaceed Cherry Cream Filling, 113
glaze
    Chocolate Glaze, 113
Great Grandma's Ginger Cookies, 25

H

Hazelnut Shortbread, 41
Honeydew Compote with Lime, Basil, and Mint, 144

K

Karen's Classic Pecan Pie, 66
Key Lime Mousse, 138

L

Lemon Bars, 43
Lemon Bread with Lemon Glaze, 121
Lemon Cream Cheese Frosting, 112
Lemon Custard, 133
Light Pumpkin Pie, 74

M

Macadamia Coconut Bars, 44
Maple Bread Pudding, 132
Marinated Strawberries in Orange Liqueur, 146
Mile High Pie, 71
Mint Chocolate Brownies, 35
Mississippi Mud Cake, 84
Mocha Frosting, 109
Mocha Fudge Pudding Cake, 93
Mock Mince Pie, 54
Molasses Cookies, 24

N

New England Maple Cookies, 13

O

Oatmeal Chocolate Squares, 38
Old-Fashioned Applesauce Cake, 103

Old World Gingerbread, 118
Orange Chantilly Cream, 114
Orange and Kiwi Compote with
    Strawberry Sauce, 144
Orange Shortbread, 41
Out of This World Spice Bars, 37

P

Peach/Apple Crisp, 79
Peach Upside-Down Cake, 99
Peaches and Raspberries in Spiced
    White Wine, 145
Peanut Butter Cookies, 14
Peanutty Chocolate Cookies, 15
Pear, Ginger, & Golden Raisin Pie, 56
Pear Pie with Ginger, Pepper, &
    Lemon, 58
Pecan & White Chocolate Chip
    Oatmeal Cookies, 20
Pie Crust, 47
pies, 45
    Amaretto Pumpkin Pie, 75
    Berry Pie, 73
    Brandied Fruit Pie, 62
    Chocolate Chunk Pecan Pie, 67
    Chocolate Mousse Pie, 72
    Classic American Apple Pie, 50
    Crustless Coconut Pecan Pie, 70
    Deep Dish Peach Pie, 59
    Dutch Apple Raisin Pie, 52
    Ginger Peach Pie, 60
    Karen's Classic Pecan Pie, 66
    Light Pumpkin Pie, 74
    Mile High Pie, 71
    Mock Mince Pie, 54
    Pear, Ginger, & Golden Raisin Pie,
        56
    Pear Pie with Ginger, Pepper, &
        Lemon, 58
    Pineapple-Glazed Apple Pie, 53
    Sweet Potato Pecan Pie, 64
    Sweet Potato Spice Pie, 63
    Texas Pecan Pie, 68
    Vinegar Pie, 49
Pineapple-Glazed Apple Pie, 53

Pineapple Upside-Down Cake, 100
Poached Pears, 142
Poached Pears with Caramel Sauce,
    143
Poppy Seed Cake with Cream
    Cheese Frosting, 97
Poppy Seed Cookies, 11
Pound Cake, 105
Pumpkin Nut Bread, 122

R

Raspberries with Ruby Port and
    Cream, 149
Rice Pudding with Dried Cherries,
    134

S

Salt-Free, Fat-Free Pineapple Cake,
    98
Sour Cream Chocolate Cake, 88
Southern Banana Bread, 126
Southern Brown Sugar Cookies, 12
Spice Cookies, 23
Spiced Carrot Cake, 95
Spicy Shortbread, 41
Strawberries and Raspberries in a
    Custard Sauce, 147
Super Easy Shortbread, 39
Super Rich Chocolate Brownies, 32
Sweet Potato Pecan Pie, 64
Sweet Potato Spice Pie, 63

T

Texas Pecan Pie, 68

V

Vanilla Frosting, 9
Vinegar Pie, 49

W

White Chocolate Chip Cookies with
    Macadamia Nuts, 21
Whole Wheat Pie Crust, 48

Notes

Notes

Notes

BOOKS BY THE CROSSING PRESS

The Balanced Diet Cookbook: Easy Menus and Recipes for Combining Carbohydrates, Proteins and Fats
By Bill Taylor

This cookbook provides simple recipes, complete menu plans, and food charts for followers of the Zone plan and others interested in balanced eating for better health.

$16.95 • Paper • ISBN 0-89594-874-5

Bill Taylor Cooks Chicken
By Bill Taylor

As the former Corporate Chef at The Crossing Press, Bill Taylor has prepared hundreds of chicken dishes and has chosen the very best for this book.

$12.95 • Paper • ISBN 1-58091-045-9

Easy & Hot from the Oven
By Elaine Goldman Gill and Bill Taylor

For the stressed parent or worn-out worker, this book presents simple recipes that rely on the oven to do the work, while still providing delicious and nourishing homemade meals. Recipes include Oven-Baked Macaroni and Cheese, Baked Sea Bass, Thai Chicken Strips, Curried Vegetable Casserole, and many more.

$12.95 • Paper • ISBN 1-58091-075-0

Everyday Tofu: From Pancakes to Pizza
By Gary Landgrebe

This book offers all Americans an opportunity to incorporate tofu into their everyday diets. We are not asking them to change their habits. We say sincerely that Americans who have remained aloof from the tofu craze will honestly be pleased by these recipes which combine tofu with their favorite foods and seasonings to create Western style main dishes, breads, and desserts.

$12.95 • Paper • ISBN 1-58091-047-5

The Great Barbecue Companion
By Bruce Bjorkman

A collection of sauces covering the best barbecue flavors: sweet, savory, hot, and spicy — sometimes mixing all four. A mouth-watering array of recipes...add this one to your library.—National Barbecue News

$12.95 • Paper • ISBN 0-89594-806-0

Good Food: The Comprehensive Food & Nutrition Resource
By Margaret M. Wittenberg

An exceptionally well-organized, up-to-date, and easily accessible treatise on food and nutrition. Wittenberg delineates a direct connection between food and quality of life.—Susan Jane Cheney, Food Writer/Columnist

$18.95 • Paper • ISBN 0-89594-746-3

BOOKS BY THE CROSSING PRESS

Innovative Soy Cooking

By Trudie Burnham

This collection of recipes is perhaps the most original kitchen work that has crossed our Editor's desk in a long time. Here are tofu, tempeh and miso dishes we drooled over!

$6.95 • Paper • ISBN 0-89594-962-8

Japanese Vegetarian Cooking

By Patricia Richfield

Easy-to-follow directions, information on techniques, plus a glossary of Japanese ingredients make this a must-have cookbook for all Japanese food fans.

$14.95 • Paper • ISBN 0-89594-805-2

Jerk: Barbecue from Jamaica

By Helen Willinsky

An inspired collection of fiery recipes from the Caribbean islands written by an expert on the topic.—Gourmet Retailer

After reading her descriptions I wanted to grab my passport and catch a plane.—Chile Pepper

$12.95 • Paper • ISBN 0-89594-439-1

Marinades: Dry Rubs, Pastes & Marinades for Poultry, Meat, Seafood, Cheese & Vegetables

By Jim Tarantino

The most comprehensive book available! Tarantino recreates marinades and flavoring pastes from all over the world, and provides instructions for preparing seafood, poultry, meat, vegetables, and cheese-indoors and out.

$16.95 • Paper • ISBN 0-89594-531-2

Noodle Fusion: Asian Pasta Dishes for Western Palates

By Andrea Chesman and Dorothy Rankin

This book has it all: from spring rolls to egg rolls, wontons to pot stickers; from cool salads to comforting soups; from vegetarian delights to deep sea wonders; from chicken and duck, to beef and pork exotica. Included is a clear description of the various Asian noodles, both fresh and dried, which are available in their astonishing array at most supermarkets.

$16.95 • Paper • ISBN 0-89594-956-3

BOOKS BY THE CROSSING PRESS

Old World Breads

By Charel Scheele

In this authentic collection, the art of old world bread-making is available to everyone. Instructions are given to get brick oven results from an ordinary oven using a simple clay flower-pot saucer. Charel Scheele was born into a Dutch family of bakers and worked as a professional baker in New York City.

$6.95 • Paper • ISBN 0-89594-902-4

Pestos!: Cooking with Herb Pastes

By Dorothy Rankin

An inventive and tasteful collection-it makes the possibilities of herb pastes enticing.—Publishers Weekly

$8.95 • Paper • ISBN 0-89594-180-5

Salad Dressings

By Teresa H. Burns

This little book is full of creative dressings that are fresh, healthy and delicious.

$6.95 • Paper • ISBN 0-89594-895-8

Sauces for Pasta!

By K. Trabant with A. Chesman

This little book has my favorite new and old sauces.—Grace Kirschenbaum, World of Cookbooks

$8.95 • Paper • ISBN 0-89594-403-0

Secrets of a Jewish Baker, 1994 James Beard award winner

By George Greenstein

... Greenstein's book is easily worth several times its price. —Vogue

$16.95 • Paper • ISBN 0-89594-605-X

Truffles, Candies, and Confections

By Carole Bloom

...Bloom has the rare ability to clearly explain technical procedures and write a recipe that's easy to follow.—Los Angeles Times

$14.95 • Paper • ISBN 0-89594-833-8

To receive a current catalog from The Crossing Press
please call toll-free, 800-777-1048.
Visit our Web site: **www.crossingpress.com**